Holy Hustle is about living life from a plac[e]  of striving. It's about realizing life is mo[re]
[about serving oth]ers than being served. It's realizing the dr[eam]
[given to you]years ago has been given to you for a divine purpose. *Holy Hustle* helps us see that no matter what job we have, what title we've been given…all our work can have a kingdom impact when we work and serve with surrendered hearts.

—Angela Perritt,
founder of LoveGodGreatly and coauthor of *You Are Loved*

This message is becoming my anthem as I grow a new ministry while I raise my children, love my husband, and serve my community, and…*Holy Hustle* is an invitation to choose another way, a better way, to success. Crystal calls us to resist our urge to strive and replace it with a desire to do God's good work, finding freedom to thrive no matter what that looks like for our unique story and season.

—Jess Wolstenholm,
coauthor of *The Pregnancy Companion* and
The Baby Companion and founder of Gather & Grow.

Hustle has never been a problem for me. It's the holy (or resting) part that remains difficult. But over the last few years I've been attempting what Crystal finally gave a perfect definition to: holy hustle—the God-intended balance between pursuing purposeful work and rejuvenating rest. Personally, I flew through this book, highlighting paragraphs on nearly every page…it was that good!

—Rachel C. Swanson,
bestselling author and speaker; accredited life coach

Holy Hustle is the road map for those of us who've heard the phrase "work-life balance" and thought it was a joke. Crystal's wisdom is sincere and encouraging as she lays out an acheivable path to work hard, love others, and rest well.

—Michelle Peterson ,
executive pastor of campuses, communication, and
leadership development at Great Lakes Church, Wisconsin;
bestselling author of *#staymarried*

Crystal Stine is a gift. I love her heart behind *Holy Hustle*. I so agree with Crystal as she explains that we give our best to the work the Lord has given us to do, and we marvel as He takes our flawed efforts and brings forth fruit that only He can. You will love this book!

—Alli Worthington,
author of *Fierce Faith*

From a young age, I considered *slacker* a far worse insult than *workaholic*. Believed that God condemned relaxation while condoning overwork. Considered *work-life balance* absurd fantasy and dismissed *doing nothing* as a contradiction in terms. Oh, to have met Crystal before midlife found me burned-out, bewildered, and bitter. She's the perfect blend of reassuring friend and challenging mentor all-or-nothing gals like me need!

Through the pages of *Holy Hustle,* Crystal will equip you to strive less and serve more. You'll receive permission—and admonition—to do only what you're actually called to do. Learn how to exchange exhaustion for excitement, comparison for community. And you'll finally find the unique balance of holy and hustle God created you for.

—Cheri Gregory,
coauthor of *Overwhelmed* and
You Don't Have to Try So Hard

CRYSTAL STINE

HARVEST HOUSE PUBLISHERS
EUGENE, OREGON

Holy Hustle
Copyright © 2018 Crystal Stine
Published by Harvest House Publishers
Eugene, Oregon 97408
www.harvesthousepublishers.com

ISBN 978-0-7369-7296-3 (pbk.)
ISBN 978-0-7369-7297-0 (eBook)

Library of Congress Cataloging-in-Publication Data is on file at the Library of Congress, Washington, DC.

Printed in the United States of America

18 19 20 21 22 23 24 25 26 / VP-SK / 10 9 8 7 6 5 4 3 2

To Matt and Madi,
for always believing in me.

These words would not exist without
your encouragement, love, and prayers.

You are my greatest blessings
and the best parts of my story.

Contents

Foreword

When Crystal invited me to write the foreword to this book, I was honored but wondered whether I was qualified to lend my voice to a message about the healthy balance of hustle and rest. At the time, I was months into a solid stretch of non-stop work trying to build my business—juggling new product collections, client design projects, and writing requests, all of which required more time, resource, creativity, thought, and planning than I had anticipated.

In that intense season of deadlines, commitments, and projects, I left little margin in my life for the God-given gift of rest. I didn't feel I had much of a choice except to power through to get it all done. I knew God had given me a measure of grace to carry the heavy workload for a time, but I also recognized there was a responsibility on my part not to allow myself to be drawn into the trap of striving to work fast and furious in my own strength.

It didn't take but a few sentences into *Holy Hustle* to feel that this timely message was a breath of fresh air. I had experienced how easily we can find ourselves drawn into unsustainable and out-of-balance habits in order to accomplish what is before us to do. We may even try to excuse our decision to press through and keep up the pace in the name of faithfully serving in our calling, even though God has invited us to approach that holy calling in a better way. Knowing God promises to give rest and to provide for those He loves (Psalm 127:2), we have to be diligent to remain in that place of grace to do our best work as unto Him, and also to rest well in His grace, timing, and provision.

The message of *Holy Hustle* isn't that intense seasons of work are wrong or unnecessary. Rather, it's that we need to be mindful to accept the grace and gift of rest alongside our faithful acts of work and service in the way God demonstrated and designed. When those things collide, that's what *Holy Hustle* looks like.

If you have found yourself in a place where the work feels too overwhelming to manage on your own, there is good news. God's strength is made perfect and full in our limitations. The message in this book isn't meant to point out where we've come up short or where we've missed the mark but to encourage and affirm that our work is indeed honorable, noble, worthwhile, and meaningful. It's a good thing to be a hard worker, but even more so, it's a grace-filled God-thing to do it without striving, to be obedient to do what God has called us to do, and to lay down the things He has not called us to do.

As we journey through this book with Crystal, I pray we will lean into the "work-hard, rest-well" design God intended. As we do, we will become well positioned to live our lives to the fullest; serve our family, friends, and community; be fruitful and successful in our calling; make a lasting kingdom impact; and bring honor and glory to God.

—Andrea Howey
   Artist and founder of Andrea Howey & Co

Introduction

found my daughter at my desk the other morning, cartoons playing on the iPad while she pretended to "work like Mommy." Although a few years ago her preschool class looked at me blankly when I tried to explain my job as a freelance writer on Career Day, she loves that I work from home. Her desk in her room is set up to reflect mine, and she comes in frequently to borrow staplers, tape, and sticky notes as she works on her own books. Her stories, illustrated with stick figures (I always have a triangle on my head to represent my faux hawk hairstyle), consist of the adventures our family takes. But isn't that what the best books do? Invite you to join in the special moments of everyday life?

Madison, who is six years old and getting ready to start first grade, loves that her mommy writes books. She sees the huge sticky notes on my wall and tracks my progress, asking me to read her the chapter titles of *Holy Hustle* and cheering for me when I complete a new section. My girl is my mini-me in so many ways. She is creative, inspired by beautiful sunsets, and loves chocolate. Her big brown eyes look just like mine, and she craves good stories, big hugs, and encouraging words. She wants to be a teacher, an artist, a writer, and a mommy when she grows up, and when Madi puts her mind to something, no one can stop her.

Stubborn? Maybe. Persistent? Without a doubt.

Holy hustle is the legacy I hope to leave her—the story of my life, God's work in my heart, and lessons for working hard and resting well.

I hope she learns those lessons far earlier than I did. This is the story God has developed in me over more than ten years, a mural created out of brokenness, failure, and shame, now turned into something that looks incomprehensibly different. Those pieces of my story I wanted to hide have been transformed into a story of hope and contentment, and a new definition of success.

In this book, we'll unpack why holy hustle is different from the world's view of hustle, how we can choose serving over striving, and what God says about work and rest. We'll also discover how we can apply the lessons we learn to our lives. I hope you have a pen, a highlighter, and a notebook or a journal nearby. As you read, highlight sentences, write in the margins, answer the questions, and fold down the corners. This book is meant to be used well.

In each chapter, you'll hear part of my story, and then we'll dig deeper into Scripture. Whether you read your Bible on your phone, on your computer, or in a physical book, you'll want to have it handy to get the most out of those sections.

And then because my voice is just one I pray will encourage you from these pages, I'll share a holy hustle story from a woman who inspires me. I want you to hear from some women who are walking with us as we make room in our lives for work *and* rest. You'll find a variety of stages of life, levels of influence, and job titles.

Here's an example of what to expect, from my friend Amanda:

God has taught me *hustle* is not a bad word by allowing me the grace of working alongside hard-working, Jesus-loving teammates who do excellent work for His glory and not their own. The more challenging a problem or project, the more we dig in—together—and give our best efforts to achieve the best result. My team has taught me that a dedicated, diligent work ethic can be a means of grace: we give our best to the work the Lord has given us to do, and we marvel as He takes our flawed efforts and brings forth fruit that only He can. Holy hustle, for me, means working hard and resting hard—and trusting the Lord in both. When I need help maintaining that balance, I turn to two scriptures:

> Unless the LORD builds a house,
> its builders labor over it in vain;
> unless the LORD watches over a city,
> the watchman stays alert in vain.
> In vain you get up early and stay up late,
> working hard to have enough food—
> yes, He gives sleep to the one He loves (Psalm 127:1-2).
>
> God, who is rich in mercy, because of His great love that He had for us, made us alive with the Messiah even though we were dead in trespasses. You are saved by grace! Together with Christ Jesus He also raised us up and seated us with him in the heavens, so that in the coming ages He might display the immeasurable riches of His grace through His kindness to us in Christ Jesus. For you are saved by grace through faith, and this is not from yourselves; it is God's gift—not from works, so that no one can boast (Ephesians 2:4-9).

I hope you'll see your story and a new way to view hustle as you read these stories from women who have been called to do many different types of work. After each holy hustle story, we'll take some time to reflect on what we've just discussed, and you'll have time to ask God what He wants to do with this journey in your life.

The voices from these pages are not from experts. We are all simply friends making room at the table for you to join the conversations. Your work, whatever it looks like, matters because God has created you to do it for His glory and His kingdom.

You belong here.

1

The Redemption of Hustle

*We often miss opportunity because it's
dressed in overalls and looks like work.*

THOMAS A. EDISON

Hustle works 24/7, jogging along in high heels on busy city streets with a coffee in one hand, a phone in the other, ignoring everyone around her. She is ruthless about getting the job done and will do whatever it takes to make sure she shines brighter than the rest, even if it means pulling an all-nighter to finish another presentation or missing time with her family. Hustle believes she can do it on her own if she simply works harder, does more, says yes to everything. She doesn't need anyone else to help her because she knows she has what it takes.

Holy takes long quiet walks in prayer labyrinths and devours books on soul-care, self-care, and grace. She wakes up early to spend no less than 30 minutes in her quiet-time chair, stocking up on scented candles and buying Bibles with extra wide margins for journaling. Holy doesn't understand why Hustle can't slow down and rest, and Hustle doesn't understand why Holy seems to be missing the opportunity to serve her family and community through work.

What if there was another way to live? A place where we can find ourselves embracing the work God has given us while honoring His command to rest—holy hustle?

The message of holy hustle isn't intended to pile on criticism, doubt, or anxiety. Based on Scripture and with examples of spiritual men and women as our guide, this message is meant to affirm, encourage, and challenge us—not to do more, but to live more.

Tucked into holy hustle is freedom that takes away the guilt of work and the shame of rest.

Before we dive in any further, let's rest our hearts in the Psalms: "My help and glory are in God—granite-strength and safe-harbor-God. So trust him absolutely, people; lay your lives on the line for him. God is a safe place to be" (Psalm 62:7 MSG).

As we say, "Hello, hustle," we need to be fully committed to saying, "Good-bye, striving." The line between holy hustle and striving is thin. Striving puts all the pressure, responsibility, and results on us. Striving says, "You're in control and it's up to you to make it right." The kind of hustle we're talking about wants nothing to do with striving, working 24/7, ignoring our families, or doubting the impact we'll have as we faithfully pursue our work. This hustle—holy hustle—says, "You aren't enough, so make room for God to do the new things He has planned for your life." Holy hustle doesn't put pressure on us to perform; it invites us to a deeper relationship with the only One who can turn our small offerings into great gifts.

◇◇◇◇◇

If you ever need to find me on a typical evening, look no further than the comfortable spot on my sofa. It's the spot on the left, perfectly worn in with two pillows. You'll find a soft blanket there, and nearby on the floor, a cup of tea and a snack. In my current season of life as a self-employed, work-from-home boss-mama (who enjoys an excellent hyphenated title, apparently), bedtime for my daughter means it's time to relax doing something my husband and I both love: watching television. In separate rooms. We learned long ago that the secret to success and happiness in our marriage requires two unique but essential elements:

1. We can't use the self-checkout at the grocery store together.

2. Apart from football on a Sunday afternoon and the Food Network Channel, it's best if we watch TV separately.

I love my husband dearly, but not his excitement to watch CNN, ESPN, or *Independence Day* for the eight hundredth time. Likewise, although he's chased after my heart since we were seniors in high school, he can't fathom why anyone would want to watch reality television, *Project Runway*, or a Christmas movie on the Hallmark Channel in October.

A few months ago I was watching *Shark Tank*, the TV series that invites entrepreneurs and inventors to display their products to a panel of incredibly successful businesspeople who appear to have nothing better to do than spend a few hours investing in the next great socks line. From QVC executives to the occasional actor, the *Shark Tank* experts have made their millions (or billions) and are looking to offer financial support and business guidance to a few lucky folks just starting out—in exchange for a nice portion of their business.

I don't remember who was on the show that night or what they had invented, but I remember hearing expert Mark Cuban share that it took him ten years to become an overnight success.

I laughed when I heard that, but I haven't been able to forget it. In our culture, each of us can curate the beautiful highlights of our lives we want to share with the world on social media, and the people we follow can do the same. That means we usually see only the end of their story. We breathe a sigh of relief when we hear someone famous admit that the end of her story—the culmination of her hustle, drive, success, failure, change of direction, and passion—wasn't achieved the way we've come to expect.

Far too often we find ourselves filling in the blanks about how "they" got to where they are and assume it came quickly for them. Think about the person you follow on Instagram who does what you would love to do one day. What story have you written for them? Have you been watching them long enough to see the slow rise, the hard work, the quiet times when nothing seemed to go right? Or have you assumed some secret tribe of internet bosses discovered them and simply handed them the opportunity to be successful?

We get frustrated when we spend days, weeks, and months putting in hard, unseen work for what we assume was gifted to someone else, but we never take the time to hear their story. Have you ever wondered…

- If they worked hard and unseen for years?
- How they suffered before they succeeded?
- How their faith grew or how God answered their prayers— or how He hasn't responded to some yet?

We see fame and opportunity, and we covet it. But in a world where we can pass judgment or connect with someone with the double-tap of a finger on a square photo on Instagram, we miss the story.

I don't want to miss the story anymore. And I don't want to be afraid to tell my story for fear that my hustle will cause someone to judge me. There's that word again: *hustle.* When I look at the men and women I follow on social media, the books I read, and the messages I hear, two camps seem to exist when it comes to this word:

- The world shouts at us to hustle harder than ever and not worry about who we crush along the way.
- The church yells at us to stop hustling altogether and to embrace rest, soul-care, and grace.

Together, the six letters in the word *hustle* seem so divisive, and we feel it, don't we? We struggle to balance in our hearts the way God created us to work hard alongside the shame we feel when our work looks like "hustle." At the end of the day, *hustle* is simply a word that exemplifies hard work and effort, but I bet many of us would define it differently. Does "ceaselessly striving" sound familiar? Maybe you also love to work but feel as though working hard is wrong and less honorable than rest. Is it hard to be proud of the work you do and the work God is doing through you because hustle isn't something you want to admit doing?

What if we could redeem hustle?

The phrase *holy hustle* has been rolling around in my head for a long time because it seems to bridge those two "all or nothing" camps. I don't want to be the kind of woman who strives unnecessarily toward my agenda. I don't want sleepless nights or endless stress. But I do want to work as hard as I can on whatever God gives me to do. There is something beautifully holy and redeeming about that kind of work, where our titles and positions are not for our personal glory, but to magnify God in the spheres of influence where He's placed us.

The discovery of holy hustle is the journey God has taken me on for more than ten years. (I guess Mark Cuban and I have something in common.) Together we'll discover what it means to work without shame, and rest without guilt, leaning into the balance God so graciously shows us in His Word.

But first we need to redeem the word *hustle* and recognize how God has uniquely created us to use those talents for His glory.

God has given each of us roles that include—but are certainly not limited to—wife, mom, friend, coworker, manager, coach, or _____ (insert your unique role). I'm learning that I don't have the kind of personality to sit back and calmly breathe, assuming someone else will take care of the work that needs to be done. In fact, at a recent training, I discovered that God wired me to be primarily responsible and strategic. Aren't those the two most exciting adjectives? I'm the life of the party! However, when something needs to be done, I get it done. If it needs a plan, I'll make one in a color-coded spreadsheet. Hustle is built into my DNA the same way my eye color is—and I'm learning that it can either be my downfall or used for God's glory.

More than 20 years ago, I sat at my desk in a seventh-grade liberal arts class near the front of the room. This class was where I could be creative. In an everyday, school-assigned journal that looked the same on the outside as every other journal in the class, I could be myself. The pages were covered with handwritten stories, book reports, newspaper articles, and interviews. The smell of pencil, the sound as it scratched words as quickly as it could grab them from my head, and the ability to lose track of time in the world I was creating were magical.

One day I opened my journal to find a note written at the top of my most recent assignment. "You are a great writer. Would you like to join the school newspaper?" My heart jumped into my throat. It was the first time I could remember being invited to do something because of my talent. As an identical twin, my identity had been wrapped up in the oddly unique fact that I looked, sounded, and acted exactly like someone else. I was unique for not being unique at all.

But this invitation? It was just for me, not because anyone felt obligated to include me if they invited my sister. It was mine. I took the role seriously, determined to interview the most engaging faculty in the school. I bought a recorder to make my interviews official, reporting hard-hitting news about upcoming events and school lunch changes.

My middle school journalism career may have lasted only a few months, and I certainly didn't win any awards for my writing, but God planted a seed with that invitation that has grown into something much larger. I learned that I'm my most joyful when I'm doing the work God created for me, living in those talents and passions.

My childhood dreams of a lifelong career as the managing editor for a fancy magazine in New York City never became a reality. And although my journey to discover who God made me has taken more twists and turns than this Type A planner would ever care to experience, God has graciously continued to grow the seed He planted long ago.

Several months ago I was going through yet another unexpected job transition. At church that morning we flipped (or tapped, or swiped, depending on our Bible app) to the book of Ruth. I was in the midst of a pity party for myself and feeling like a failure when we paused to read Ruth's story. I almost tuned out, having heard her story repeatedly. I'd done whole studies on this book of the Bible; surely there wouldn't be anything new. And yet, as God so often does with His living and active Word, a fresh perspective appeared, speaking to my doubts about work and worth and my questions about success and striving.

Ruth was, by all accounts, faithful, loyal, and trusting. But this day, God showed me how Ruth also hustled. When she and Naomi needed to find food, Ruth laced up her boots (figuratively) and went to the field. She worked hard, harder than most of the others there. Ruth stopped for breaks when she needed them, but kept going even when it was challenging. She trusted God, did the work He called her to do, and was rewarded for it.

That's the kind of hustle I want to have. The kind that trusts God's agenda over mine and does everything to serve His kingdom instead of building one for myself. It's the holy hustle that has given me a love for writing and creativity, and for inviting more women to join me on this journey. It's what keeps me motivated to share encouragement and inspiration on social media, and what doesn't allow my brain to stop dreaming up new ideas, businesses, stories, and ways to offer resources that equip women.

Around our house, *hustle* isn't a scary word. It's just what I do.

When we look at the dictionary definition of hustle, all it means is to "work rapidly or energetically."[1] Doesn't it remind you of Colossians 3:23? "Whatever you do, work at it with all your heart, as working for the Lord, not for human masters" (NIV). When I feel guilty about working hard and attempt to follow the models of rest and soul-care that seem to be popular right now, I find myself leaning too heavily into laziness. When I turn too far the other way and work nonstop, following the world's definition of hustle, I find myself striving and exhausted. Either way, I end up feeling miserable.

We serve a God who created the entire earth and everything on it out of nothing in six days. God modeled work for us—energetic, creative, hard work followed by rest. As I've prayed about how this model fits with the concept of modern hustle, God has revealed a few things:

1. Hustle isn't bad when we work hard for what glorifies God and serves His kingdom.

2. Scripture provides examples of the blessing of hard work.

3. We can't live 100 percent of our lives modeled after the first six days of creation and ignore day seven.

Hustling doesn't have to mean getting ahead, walking all over our coworkers, or shining a spotlight on ourselves. Holy hustle is about working hard the way Colossians 3:23 commands, living fully in the lane where God has placed us and discovering the restorative balance of work and rest.

While we're redeeming hustle, can we also be done with the myth of the overnight success? Of course, some people find themselves in the middle of overnight fame (I'm looking at you, 2016 Chewbacca mask lady), have a viral blog post one day, or do something that makes the news. But I don't think we're created to sustain that kind of life.

We're designed to work hard, to hustle after the holy things that bring God glory, and to connect meaningfully with others. And that takes time. It takes boring, ordinary, everyday, unseen work. It takes believing that God will continue to work in and through us—right where we are—until He sees fit to call our work on earth complete.

As we journey together and figure out what constitutes holy hustle, I challenge you to take the time to learn about the real stories behind the people you admire.

Let's invest in learning, not assuming,
so we can be encouraging, not envious.

Let's do the work in front of us and trust that God will do what He wants with it to bring glory to Himself, not to us.

Digging Deeper

Read Colossians 3

Before we get started, will you do me a favor? Grab your Bible and read Colossians 3. The rest of this chapter will make so much more sense if you're reading with a Bible open beside you. We'll do this in each chapter, so keep that Bible nearby!

Scripture is packed full of examples of work. We read about the kind of work we're to focus on, the attitude we should have when we do it, and what happens to us when we fail to follow the model God has planned for us. In the book of Colossians, Paul writes to the church in Colossae to "correct the false teachings that were cropping up in the church. In doing so, Paul presented a clear picture of Jesus Christ as the supreme Lord of the universe, head of the church, and the only One through whom forgiveness is possible."[2] Following Paul's chapters on theological instruction, he moves on to several sections encouraging believers to live the kind of life that comes after Christ has entered into our lives and fully transformed us. We're no longer bound to "the way things have always been," but are given the freedom to pursue life the way God intends.

Early in chapter 3 (especially verses 5 through 10), Paul gives the believers in Colossae—and us—a list of the old ways we are to put to death. Viewed through the lens of work and hustle, "greed" feels particularly relevant to our discussion. If you look at your intentions, goals, and motivations behind the work you do, does an element of greed stand out? In the world's pursuit of hustle, there certainly is an element of greed as we watch the competition for more fame, more platforms, more opportunities, more titles, more income.

We are bombarded by messages every day that tell us we need/deserve "more." Around the holidays commercials tell my daughter she needs every latest and greatest toy, showing her pictures of smiling children with a lot of friends, making her believe that to feel welcomed and included, she just needs *more*. She starts to sound like the birds in *Finding Nemo* every time we go to a store: "Mine! Mine! Mine! Mine!"

As her parents, we know the holidays are a good time to limit our access to television and refocus on what matters most. We tell her often that people are more important than programs, and that it's good and right to stop doing something you love to help someone in need. We talk about what it means to be grateful for everything we already have. We also talk about why it's okay to appreciate beautiful new things, but how our lives would feel empty if we filled them with more things and fewer people.

"Do as I say, not as I do" at its finest, right there.

As adults, our desire for more only gets louder and more expensive. We're shown why we need a more expensive car, a fancier house, the newest clothing, and the best of everything—because *then* we'll feel like we've achieved all our dreams. Friends will invite us over, our boss will see we're worth the promotion, and everything will be wrapped in such a beautiful package of *more* that we'll be happy—right?

Success isn't about having or doing more;
success is about serving more.

As the world shouts "More!" at us, we dive into our work. We work more and rest less to make the kind of money that will buy us more, or will get us out of the debt into which we've fallen. Greed ranks up there on Paul's list, which includes "evil desires" and "sexual immorality," and yet we find ourselves so often brushing away the nagging thought that maybe more isn't better. We know we would never fall into any of those other areas Paul tells us to put to death, so we skim over "greed" and move on to the part of the chapter we like, where he says we are loved, chosen, and holy (Colossians 3:12).

We are all three of those things and so much more in the eyes of God, but to truly embrace a life of holy hustle we need to stop and see where we've gone wrong. Could it be greed has pushed us into working long, striving hours? Could it be greed that sets the stage for jealousy and envy when a coworker or friend receives the role you wanted so badly?

As we go further through Colossians chapter 3, Paul encourages the believers in Colossae. We need that encouragement right now, don't we? That first part was tough, and we need a hug. That's where Paul comes in at verse 12 with his reminder that, although the believers have been making some profound mistakes, their work isn't over. God isn't done with them, and He's not done with us either.

Now we're to move forward with compassion, kindness, humility, gentleness, and patience (3:12). We're to forgive, put on love, let the peace of Christ control our hearts, and be thankful (3:13-15). We're to refocus our work on spreading the message of Christ in all we do, "and whatever [we] do, in word or in deed, do everything in the name of the Lord Jesus, giving thanks to God the Father through Him" (3:17). It's impossible to be at once both greedy and thankful. Paul has not only pointed out what needs to be fixed, but shown us the solution: be thankful.

Matthew Henry offers this commentary on verse 17: "All must be done in the name of Christ according to his command and in compliance with his authority, by strength derived from him, with an eye to his glory."[3] When we find ourselves working according to our own command, in our own strength, with an eye toward our own glory and depending on others around us for acceptance, we have missed the point of our work entirely.

Hustle tells us we should push ourselves ahead to get more. Holy hustle tells us to work hard in the name of Jesus to make His name great, not ours.

Paul goes on to say in verses 23-24, "Whatever you do, do it enthusiastically, as something done for the Lord and not for men, knowing that you will receive the reward of an inheritance from the Lord. You serve the Lord Christ." The context indicates he was writing to the slaves in the households of Colossae who struggled to have a strong work ethic, but this portion of the chapter is just as much for you today. As you wash the dishes for the fifth time that day, as you eat another boring lunch in your cubicle, as you wait in the school drop-off line or sit in traffic, as you heave a hamper of laundry up the stairs, as you talk about the weather to another customer in line. This world is a temporary home for us, and it can be a struggle to maintain a positive attitude, a healthy work/rest balance, and to do our very best when it feels as though we'll never see the rewards.

No matter what work we do, how we identify ourselves by our job titles, where we work, or how many hours each week we devote to the tasks God has given us, we need to be equally aware of our greedy nature and our laziness. Both are indicators that God's model for a healthy work/rest balance is missing from our lives. Fall too far one way, and we find ourselves striving ceaselessly. Fall too far the other way, and we find ourselves binge watching far too much Netflix and putting off the work for another day (again). Our success shouldn't be measured by the recognition we receive here on earth, but our hearts should work enthusiastically, hustling in the work God has given us because we have faith in the reward we'll receive in heaven.

When we know every hair on our head has been counted by the God who created us (Matthew 10:30), we can believe He sees the work we do. It does not go unnoticed by the One who matters most, regardless of how quiet, behind the scenes, or small it feels compared to what anyone else in our circles is doing. It's up to us to wake up each morning and focus our whole hearts on the work set before us, whether or not anyone sees us do it.

Holy hustle comes not from working ourselves to exhaustion but from excitedly working for the Lord.

Whether the work happens in your household, at an office building, in a school, at a factory, or somewhere else, God has given you the ability and opportunity to serve Him and His kingdom.

In my current season as a self-employed freelance writer, I often find myself wondering if the work I do makes a difference. I sit at home by myself, and at the end of the day, I don't have a pile of widgets to prove I've done anything important. I spend a lot of my time on social media for work and personal projects, and I see where others are thriving when I struggle to feel like I'm surviving. I wonder if I should be "there" or do "that" or run my business more like "her."

One morning I asked God, "Why not me?" after seeing someone receive something I had worked hard toward. He graciously showed me why He needs me right where I am.

Imagine that you're in the middle of a large arena, on stage. Unlike real life, where public speaking makes your knees shake and your voice quaver, in this daydream you're ready for the spotlight to shine on you and for the seats to fill with women who have come to hear your message. The passion God has given you and the experiences and stories and lessons you've learned along the way are ready to be shared. But instead of the seats filling up, the stage fills up. Women pile onto the stage, all fighting for their place in the spotlight. You start shouting your message across the arena, working hard to be the loudest, the brightest, the main attraction. But no one is in the audience, and instead of an encouraging message that will move hearts toward Christ, it's all just noise. You're fighting for a place in the light instead of shining light into dark corners of the world where people need to hear about the hope and life we have in Jesus.

God has important plans for you. But they don't have to happen on a stage, platform, or arena. What if God has you right where He needs you to shine the light on Him in your town? What if your coworkers need you to show them that hope? What if the men and women you see at the grocery store are desperate for a kind, encouraging word? What if your local church is hungry for the message God has given you? What if your social media accounts could be a place where women find rest and joy in the middle of their ordinary, everyday struggles? What if you were called to love your neighbors, not from a stage, but through your work?

It may never make you famous, but we were never created to live in the spotlight. The reward we'll receive in heaven when we do our work enthusiastically, giving thanks and glory to God, will be far greater than any accolades or stage appearances we might experience on earth.

Holy Hustle Story

You are not on this journey alone. I hope you'll have at least one "me too!" moment as you hear how God has redeemed hustle in the lives of the women sharing their lives in these pages.

CLARE: FITNESS INSTRUCTOR

I think hustle was redeemed for me when I accepted the fact that God had indeed created and wired me with this particular personality, to work hard, stand up for what I believe in, and encourage others in the process. I used to feel bad about all that because it wasn't in line with the typical outline of a Christian woman and mom. But when I started to embrace the calling and passion for health and fitness I believe God laid on my heart as I was walking deeper with Him, I began to see how all that hustle could be used for a greater purpose. That's when I threw all those cares aside and embraced the calling at any cost. I'm always open to when and if the Lord leads differently, but now I'm going all out for the kingdom!

If I had to define holy hustle in my life, I would say it's living with focused energy and determination on a God-ordained path for an eternal purpose. When I find myself leaning too far one way or the other between work and rest, I'm encouraged by this quote from Christine Caine: "I'm not trying to balance my life, but to surrender my life." Living a life of holy hustle is hard, but when we surrender to the One who gave us this work in the first place, we can bear good fruit for God's kingdom.

Reflection

It sounds like an excellent idea to redeem the word *hustle*, but what does it really mean? Before we can move on to our good-bye party for striving, we need to develop a new way of thinking, a change in how we view work, recognizing some mistakes we've made and leaning into the new things God promises to do in our lives. It's a lot. But on the other side of this new way of thinking is freedom. Freedom to find joy in the work we've been given, freedom from jealousy, and freedom to work hard without shame and to rest comfortably without guilt.

Go ahead and grab your notebook or journal or use the space at the end of this chapter and write down what your typical day or week looks like. What work do you do? How much do you rest? Do you feel like your work and busyness contribute to your overall mission and the calling God has given you in this season? Once you've had time to evaluate where you are, write down the answers to these questions that might help you see where you're going.

- In what ways are you starting to think differently about the word *hustle*?

- What motivations for your work has God revealed to you through this chapter that you need to remove?

- Do you find yourself more often on the side of striving ceaselessly or laziness?

Today, take the time to pray about your current work/rest balance. Ask God to reveal any places that don't line up with His plan for your life, areas where you're working too hard and resting too little, or areas where you're resting too much and working too little. Spend time writing out your goals, everything you would like to accomplish perhaps in the coming year, and then quietly offer those goals back to God.

Cross out anything He leads you to remove and add anything new He puts on your heart. Ask God to show you how you can make His name great through your work on these projects, and ask His forgiveness for the times when greed, a quest for fame, or a drive toward competition motivated you.

◇◇◇◇◇

_____

_____

_____

_____

_____

_____

_____

_____

_____

_____

_____

_____

_____

_____

_____

_____

_____

_____

_____

_____

_____

_____

A Good-bye Party for Striving

*No work is insignificant. All labor that uplifts
humanity has dignity and importance and should
be undertaken with painstaking excellence.*

MARTIN LUTHER KING JR.

come from a long line of women who worked and worked hard. From teachers to farmers, from receptionists to business owners, my ancestors passed down a legacy of work.

In my small town, you'll discover a state university that started a long time ago as a teaching college. One of the women in my legacy attended that college, back in the days when teaching was among the few professions available to women and when horse-drawn carriages took her from her home to her classroom. My great-grandmother owned a Christian book and music store in our town long before I was born, but the folks in our town who were around in those days remember it fondly.

My aunt owned a printing business in that same small town, and I remember how excited I was every time we were invited to spend the day and help. As much as I loved books, I found myself enjoying even more the process of watching pads of notepaper come together, glued, and bound, ready for sale in the small backroom of her store. Somewhere you'll find a candid black-and-white photo of my twin sister and me in that store window, playing with Barbies like we owned the place.

Now my aunt's daughter owns a vintage clothing and record store where you'll find yourself wishing you had a reason to wear a gorgeously detailed dress and end up leaving with a candle from Nashville in your bag.

I grew up with a single mama who worked to provide the best possible life for my sister and me. We would walk across the street to our babysitter's home when we were little, where a Christian family introduced us to Jesus and *Adventures in Odyssey*, and also gave me a new perspective on what to look for in a future husband. Mom worked right down the road as the administrative professional for a local construction company, a job she still has even though the location has changed. Now she's also joined the ranks of entrepreneurs in our family, opening a handmade soap company in a rental house owned by my grandparents.

I always assumed I would have a full-time career because that's the life I knew. We women work, we provide, and we contribute to the support of our families financially.

My early middle-school journalism career led to my dream of working as an editor for a magazine in New York. Because I'm older than the internet, the work I do now didn't exist, not even in my wildest dreams. God developed that early love for words and writing and combined it with my love for technology and social media in a job that gives me the ability to minister to and serve women online.

Since I had big dreams (and visions of fabulous shoes) for my first job, college was a natural next step after high school. And although I grew up in a town that boasted its own university, at 18 I wanted nothing more than to put some space between that tiny town and me. I craved my own identity, away from being one of "the twins." I wanted to see if I would be invited, find friends, and do what I loved without anyone feeling obligated to include me. So I went to Villanova University outside Philadelphia. I earned a bachelor's degree in English and a master's degree in Liberal Studies, which, for this book-loving girl, meant I read a lot of amazing books and fell in love with words in a fresh new way.

While I was there, I also fell in love with work. Not necessarily the course work, but working with high school students as a youth group volunteer at a local Presbyterian church and as a work-study turned part-time employee in the registrar's office. I loved working with students, and I felt confident that I could provide for myself through my paying job while investing in the lives of the students I volunteered to work with. I had two different kinds of work, and both were so valuable and necessary in that season.

God is good like that, isn't He? He knows us and sees us as more than one-dimensional beings with a single need, but places us in each season to fill our hearts and to do work for His kingdom.

More than ten years later, my current season looks entirely different. It's fascinating how the plans we make for ourselves can be so rooted in the legacy our parents leave for us. For the first 30 years of my life, my dreams and goals were all centered on my career. Motherhood wasn't even a consideration for me. I focused on not needing to rely on anyone, working hard to do what it took to obtain a business card with a fancy title and everything that came with it. I thought that equaled success.

Do you want to know what happened?

I did it.

I earned those degrees from Villanova University. I married my high school sweetheart. We bought a house and budgeted to purchase two new cars. We even had a gorgeous daughter after God softened our hearts toward parenthood in an unexpected and drastic way. I took the first job available to me after college, as a bank teller at a local community bank. After a year, I moved on to their marketing department as an assistant, and then when the marketing director changed, my role changed as well.

For the next several years I worked hard. I had my sights set on that title, that business card, that bit of proof that I was worth something to the world. I helped ring the closing bell at NASDAQ, joined the ranks of bank officers, and was invited to attend and run fancy meetings. I became an assistant vice president before I turned 30, and worked on important projects. From the outside it looked like all I was missing was the white picket fence.

But I was miserable. I struggled to maintain a positive attitude and found myself always striving for more. I alienated friends, spent far more time at work than with my family, and it was never enough.

And so in 2013, God began to close doors and prepare my heart to receive a blessing I never knew I wanted. I was fired from the only career I'd ever known. Suddenly life was chaotic and fearful. I didn't know why I was being asked to walk this road.

But God had a better plan.

Over the last few years, every idol I've had related to my work has been stripped away. When I first became a mother, I deeply grieved the transition from my old life to the new. I tried desperately to keep one foot in the life we had before and one foot in this new motherhood territory, and it was exhausting and impossible. For the first time in my life, I was doing something I wasn't any good at—and I was learning that, in the trial and error of motherhood, I was more likely to end up on the side of "error." The identity I had wrapped up in my career was the final piece that needed to be stripped away to push me into embracing life as the mother of a child.

When God called me to continue working full-time, but from home, I questioned Him about the challenges and emotions that came with having our little girl in day care. But He gave our hearts peace, a Christian day care we love, and a vision that *this*—this working from 8 to 5 and sharing in the provision for our family—is what God has called me to in this season of our family, and that He would redeem it.

My little girl would learn how to work hard by watching her mama, like I did by watching mine. I could release the guilt I felt. I wasn't selfish; I was obeying God. Now I've joined the ranks of my entrepreneurial ancestors and own a freelance company. I work from home while my husband works full-time as a third-grade teacher and our daughter attends school. That's what life looks like for us in this season. God is still working on my heart to find a healthy work/rest balance. I struggle to stop working when my family comes home, and I've developed a bit of a territorial issue with my home office.

But in doing a job I love, I pray my daughter will learn to chase her dreams, work hard, and obey God, wherever He calls her. I pray she'll learn from me that holy hustle means embracing the work we've been given, but finding our worth in the One who created us to do it. I believe our work has worth and that what we do to serve God, our neighbors, and our families is important—but that's not what defines us. I believe the work we do in every season has a reason far beyond what we can see. God doesn't make mistakes about where He places us, and He has a plan for us to do work for His kingdom, right where we are.

Scripture has quite a bit to say about the worth of work:

- Paul wrote to the Ephesians with the reminder that God has prepared good works for His children and that we have been created to do them. (Ephesians 2:10)

- In another of Paul's letters, he encouraged the Corinthians to be steadfast, working with excellence, knowing that work done for God is not done in vain. (1 Corinthians 15:58)

- The Proverbs 31 woman worked with willing hands; bought and sold land out of her earnings; created; planted; managed. (Proverbs 31:10-31)

- Deborah worked as a judge and was practically a military commander. (Judges 4–5)

Now might be a good time to grab that paper or journal and consider your thoughts, good and bad, about your work. What does your inner monologue tell you about the tasks you do every day? Do you feel like your work has value, or do you consider it "not a big deal" compared to the jobs, responsibilities, and roles of others? Do you feel like you're wasting your time staring at a computer while your family needs you, or do you worry that you're missing out on time with your family? Do you, generally speaking, feel good, bad, guilty, or indifferent about your work?

The work we do has worth when we do it to the glory of God and with a joyful heart. The time we spend doing our work isn't wasted time. God will redeem all that we fear we'll miss out on because He wastes nothing. When He calls us to work, wherever it is and whatever it looks like, it's because it's part of His plan for us, part of how He created us to serve Him and love our neighbors. But we need to be willing to say good-bye to striving.

When I was processing my job loss, a friend heard the desperation in my voice, and she prayed for me. But she also lovingly shared that I needed to stop striving so hard. I hadn't yet allowed God to remove my selfish nature in this regard, and I was still trying to make everything happen on my own. I wanted to be self-sufficient, to find ways to feel worthwhile and useful, but I wasn't giving God any room in my heart to move. I needed to throw a good-bye party to striving and welcome in a new way of life—one that put God back in control of my day.

In her book *Simply Tuesday*, Emily P. Freeman writes, "Effort is important, but I can't shake my fear of saying that. I hesitate to exalt effort because I know the tendency of my own soul to work hard to try to earn things I already have. Effort toward *excellence in my work* can silently morph into effort toward *perfection in my soul*…When I'm performing for my acceptance, burnout is always the result."[1]

God has given us quite a few names throughout Scripture—chosen, holy, loved, friends—but I have yet to find a verse that requires endless amounts of work, weeks of rest, or fancy titles on business cards to earn those names. God calls us away from striving and into a place where we can share the burden of our work with Him, making the load lighter, the work faster, and giving the glory back to God.

For some of us, saying good-bye to striving means saying no to some good things to make room for God's grand plans. My friend Myquillyn says it this way: "Saying yes to any opportunity by definition requires saying no to several others."[2] Known as "The Nester," Myquillyn had been hosting a writing challenge on her blog for six years. Each year she invited writers to join her to write for 31 days straight in the month of October for the Write 31 Days challenge. It's an amazing way to practice the habit of writing and to take the time to focus on one particular topic for an entire month.

Two years ago, Myquillyn reached out to me with a question.

Would I be interested in inheriting the Write 31 Days challenge? She was asking me to say yes so she could say no. It was an opportunity to come alongside a sister in Christ and help her create margin in her life for the next things God had planned for her. I said yes.

I know we were just talking about learning to say no and that we can't do it all. But I don't think this story contradicts that. You see, God had prepared the way for Myquillyn to say no to the challenge so He could open other doors for her. At the same time, God had been preparing me to say yes to the challenge because it was my next right thing.

God had been asking me to say no to some other good things that year so I would have room to host this challenge when the time came. He had spent a few years putting me in work positions, freelance jobs, and running community groups on the side so I would have the tools to do what needed to be done in this time. My ability to say no to good things allowed me to say yes to this one special thing God had planned—and it gave Myquillyn the chance to say no so she could make room for her next yes.

Our yeses and noes matter. We simply cannot take on everything that comes our way. When we do, when we start to strive for everything we think we *should* be doing, we lose the ability to have the work/life balance God planned for our lives.

Holy hustle means learning to say no,
and learning to ask others for help.

Joanna Weaver recounts a story that speaks to the difference between holy hustle and saying yes to every opportunity.

> There was a man who met God one day. God asked him to take a wagon with three rocks to the top of a tall mountain. The man, happy to be doing God's will, set off pulling the wagon behind him.
>
> As the man started up the base of the mountain, a friend

asked if he would mind carrying a rock for him as well. The man agreed and piled the small stone on top of the other three in his wagon.

As the man went along, more and more people asked him to take their rocks with him. Since his wagon was large and he was going to the top of the mountain anyway, he continued to load more rocks. As the wagon got fuller, it became harder to pull. As the incline of the mountain got steeper, some of the rocks started to tumble out. The man scrambled to keep all of the rocks balanced in the wagon and bear the weight of the load. Eventually, the man started to get weary and grew frustrated and resentful with the pile of rocks in his wagon. Finally, in utter despair, the man thought about just giving up and letting the wagon roll back down the hill.

The man cried out angrily to God. "You gave me a job that is too hard for me," the man sobbed. "I can't do this. It's not fair." God met the man and looked into his wagon. As the man sat nearby broken and trembling, God removed the rocks one at a time until only the three stones God had given him were left.

"Let others shoulder their own belongings," God said gently. "I know you were trying to help, but when you are weighted down with all these cares, you cannot do what I have asked of you."[3]

◇◇◇◇◇

I've developed a love for comic book characters and shows lately. Something about the battle between right and wrong, good and evil, and knowing that somehow even the most complicated and messed-up heroes always win draws me back over and over. Their struggles to say yes or no to the various demands of their dual lives, and their willingness or difficulty in asking for help from others feels particularly relevant, although their decisions typically result less in a balanced agenda than saving the planet.

Lately, I've been watching *The Flash*, which is about a character who unexpectedly developed super speed and uses it to save his friends, family, city, and the world. In one episode the show introduced a new character. She was the first female speedster on *The Flash*, and I wanted her to be amazing. I wanted her to be strong and good and sassy and powerful.

She disintegrated.

Not exactly the ending I was hoping for as I caught up on one of my favorite shows.

There was so much I wanted the speedster's character to be. So many expectations. And they created her to be a complicated mix of it all; I saw too much of myself in her. In her day-to-day life, she was smart and motivated and kind. But she was lured by power and a bit of fame. Her desire to be the best caused her to hurt others and, ultimately, herself. At the end of the story, the power she craved and collected was simply more than her physical body could handle. Despite the best efforts of the superhero team that gathered around her, they couldn't save a woman who was out of control. This self-created super speedy woman was in a state of self-destruction because she couldn't be content with the life and gifts she'd been given.

I hate to think I'm like that, but I should admit that I have been, and I can be. The tiniest bit of success can quickly convince me I need to do more, do better, be the best. I rush around to make it all happen, consumed by my own story and unable to see the people I overlook, the places I fail to serve, or the disintegration of my own heart.

We're not meant to be famous—not the way culture puts celebrities and authors and speakers and musicians on pedestals.

We're meant to make God famous.

Certain parts of my God-given personality make it a struggle to move the pendulum away from building my kingdom in my way and toward the one God wants me to build for Him. But when I stop putting myself first and I serve instead of striving, those very same gifts and personality traits can be used to draw others to God, coming alongside other talented men and women who need the very skills God has given me.

Take some time to consider your top talents and strengths. In your journal, notebook, or here in the margins, write down the gifts God has given you, giving yourself permission to accept the compliments about what you do well rather than shrugging them off.

Our talents, like any superhero movie plot, can be used for good (God) or bad (self). Unless we're ready to work ourselves into a disintegrated state of mind and soul, we need to hustle for the right things.

The holy things.

God didn't create us to "binge watch and relax," but to get busy doing good work for His kingdom on earth. When we hustle and strive to fill our lives with the things of this world, we run the risk of burning ourselves out with a never-ending desire for more. More power, more success, more fame, more recognition. But when we use the skills and talents God has given us to do the work He has called us to do, we don't strive—we thrive. We earn the ultimate recognition from the Father, "'Well done, good and faithful servant!'" (Matthew 25:21 NIV). And we give the credit and glory and fame to whom they're due, not to ourselves.

Let's chase God's best for our lives—because disintegrating didn't look all that fun.

Digging Deeper

Paul is once again at work, this time writing a letter to the believers in Ephesus. Some scholars believe Paul wrote this letter and the one to Colossae that we explored earlier at the same time.[4]

Paul begins and ends this letter with love, focusing on unity in the church, and how we become new creations when we believe in Jesus Christ. In his letter to the Colossians, Paul encouraged them to "put to death" (3:5) old ways, habits, and heart issues (like greed). Here he reminds the Ephesians of the same thing. We are no longer bound to do things the way we've always done them, or the way the world tells us we should. We are new creations with fresh starts, and we can put to death the world's version of hustle and striving and embrace holy hustle without shame.

Like the Ephesians, however, we must be reminded that none of these changes, none of the unity, can come through our strength. It is only because of the power of the Holy Spirit given to us by God that we can love well, strive less, and serve more.

When I think back on my career story and the struggles I've encountered, hindsight kindly shows me I was putting projects before people, I was striving more than I was serving, and I was hungering for fame instead of being humble and gracious. My way of hustle, and the way so many "get ahead" self-help books and speakers encourage it, caused discord, envy, and broken relationships.

God builds in us a calling and a passion for doing His work through love, which unites and strengthens His church.

When you look back at your life, does this ring true? Do you see areas where striving caused brokenness? Maybe now you struggle to find the motivation to work hard at the tasks God has given you because you fear you'll fall into those same cycles again. I get it. God is still teaching me so much, but when we hustle hard in love and gratitude, our efforts will not be in vain.

Paul reminds the Ephesians, and us, that before we were in Christ we "walked according to the ways of this world" and carried "out the inclinations of our flesh and thoughts" (Ephesians 2:2-3). But now? Oh, this is where it gets good and where we find freedom from our striving: "God, who is rich in mercy, because of His great love that He had for us, made us alive with the Messiah even though we were dead in trespasses. You are saved by grace!...For you are saved by grace through faith, and this is not from yourselves; it is God's gift—not from works, so that no one can boast. For we are His creation, created in Christ Jesus for good works, which God prepared ahead of time so that we should walk in them" (Ephesians 2:4-5,8-10).

That is good news! God knows us so well that long before we were ever on this earth, He put into motion the only way to find freedom and salvation *through a gift*. He knew we would be tempted to outdo one another with work, with hustle, with many hours spent trying to earn it all, and He did the only thing that could ever make us stop striving. He gave salvation to us as a gift. No strings attached. There is nothing we could ever do to earn it, and nothing we must do to compete with anyone else to keep it.

Grace saves us, but not to sit around and wait for someone else to serve us. God created us for a specific purpose—to do good works. Work! We are created for it, God has a plan for it, and we are the hands and feet and creative brains that get to do it. The commentary in my Bible says, "Good works are demonstrated in gratitude, character, and actions."[5] The kind of holy hustle we are created for isn't displayed to the world by how many people we climb over on the way up the corporate ladder. A grateful heart, a character that shines Jesus, and actions that serve others allow us to throw one big farewell party to striving.

Years ago, I attended my first Beth Moore Bible study. I was the youngest woman in the room, and I admit I had no idea what I was getting myself into. I'd never been in a book club, much less walked into a room full of strangers to study the Bible. I thought maybe I would sit in the back, hear a few stories, connect with a couple of new people at the church, and be on my way.

That group of women taught me to love God's Word in a way I never knew was possible. I realized that somewhere deep within that passion for words God had given me was a desire to figure out where it all came from. I loved the history behind the stories, the maps, learning how to pronounce the ancient languages, and seeing how God wove stories together with the same word or phrase over generations of text. Instead of thinking of the Bible as 66 separate and disjointed books, I found His Word becoming alive. Its stories are blended together to create a purposeful tale across history that somehow, in an incredible way, includes you and me. We're part of the story now. And in the same way that I love learning about my ancestors and discovering where my entrepreneurial spirit comes from, I love seeing God at work in the lives of men and women who had similar struggles and dreams as me. It gives me hope that, even if I don't see how it all works out, God is still at work so that I can bring rest back into my life.

The Greek word for work used in Ephesians 2 is *ergon*. Paul uses it four times in the book of Ephesians, most notably in the passages we just read together, and it's used a total of 169 times throughout the New Testament.

I'd say God has a thing or two to say about work, wouldn't you?

Here's something interesting. Another Greek term related to *ergon* is *energeia*, meaning "working, action, or activity."[6] Do you remember what our original definition of hustle was? The dictionary described it as "to work rapidly or energetically."[7] Energetically. *Energeia*. We might call it hustle, but the concept has been around for centuries. It's what we do with it that makes a difference in our lives and with those we love.

Paul uses the word *ergon* two ways in this section of Ephesians, "to deny that works or human effort contribute to salvation and to affirm that those who are saved will manifest good works."[8] We can deny striving a place in our lives and affirm that we are created to work for God's glory.

Holy Hustle Story

ERIN: MARATHON RUNNER

God redeemed hustle in a humbling way for me. When I was working hard and trying to get attention for the work I had done for my online ministries, I found very little affirmation or fulfillment. I made a small change and started doing more behind-the-scenes work, trying to be faithful in what I was asked to do, whether or not anyone noticed. Suddenly God started giving me a glimpse into how He was working through my life. I saw how people were being affected by the work I had contributed to. They had no idea I was behind it, yet that was more than enough. Serving God humbly became more refreshing and fulfilling than my striving for recognition.

It was less about me, and that was the redemption I needed. For me, holy hustle means working hard in the strength of the Lord, for His glory, and with my eyes fixed on Him. That's something I've learned in my work, as a mom, and in my marathon training. My strength comes from the Lord, not from me. When I need a reminder or help to refocus on serving rather than striving, I turn to Galatians 6:9-10:

> So let's not allow ourselves to get fatigued doing good. At the right time we will harvest a good crop if we don't give up, or quit. Right now, therefore, every time we get the chance, let us work for the benefit of all, starting with the people closest to us in the community of faith (MSG).

Reflection

I wish throwing a farewell party for striving was as easy as buying a few packs of confetti, a cake, and some balloons. Although, frankly, cake does make everything a little easier. God has shown me repeatedly that my fight against striving is a daily battle. Every time I sit down at my computer to work, I must be intentional about whom I'm serving. Every time an opportunity comes my way, I must be willing to slow down and consider whether it's my next best yes or a no that will pass that chance on to someone better equipped to pursue it. I've seen what happens when I follow the voices that scream, "But what's in it for me?" and I've been blessed by the times my heart has chosen instead to ask, "How can I serve God in this?"

Before we can create some quiet space to explore the worth of our work, we need to pull our striving out of hiding and say good-bye to it once and for all.

- Where has striving caused you to stumble?
- When you think of the word *work*, what is your initial reaction?
- Where is God asking you to stop striving?
- Have you ever experienced a time when someone said no so you could say yes?

Today, take the time to ask God to reveal which area—gratitude, character, or action—needs some attention so you can be better equipped to produce the good works He has planned for your life. If it's gratitude, make a list of the blessings you have in your life and in your work. Thank God for giving you gifts far greater than anything you could ever deserve.

If God nudges you to work on an aspect of your character, write down one action you will take this week to work on that trait and pair it with one Bible verse you'll commit to memory as you do it.

If God reveals He has called you to undertake a particular action, but you haven't yet taken the first step, write it on your calendar and prayerfully pursue where God is calling you to serve.

◇◇◇◇◇

_____

_____

_____

_____

_____

_____

_____

_____

_____

_____

_____

_____

_____

_____

_____

_____

_____

_____

_____

_____

_____

_____

_____

_____

_____

3

Called Here

Don't wait for passion to lead you somewhere you're not.
Start by bringing passion to the place where you are.

JOHN ORTBERG

May I share a secret with you? When I read books by other authors, I'm usually willing to give them three chapters to hook me, to somehow keep my attention long enough and share enough interesting stories that I just *have* to keep reading. I've been known to abandon books that make it onto "must read" lists and "bestseller" lists because, after three chapters, I'm no longer invested.

Will you do me a favor? Stick with me. If this new concept of holy hustle hasn't put you off, and the self-reflection of identifying your issues with striving hasn't made you feel too uncomfortable, this next section, I believe, will feel like a long-awaited chance to stretch your legs after a cramped car ride.

It's okay. You can stand up, stretch, maybe let out a sigh. Refill your coffee while you're up, and let's discover how quieting the noise of the world and focusing our hustle on the particular work God has called us to do—right where we are—is worth the cost.

◇◇◇◇◇

For as long as I can remember, I've been very aware of my surroundings. Not in a "know where all the exits are because you're in witness protection" kind of way (although as a child I did want to be in the FBI). And I wish it were the kind of aware that would make me brave to make eye contact with people in crowded places, like my husband's ability to walk into a room and, in 20 seconds or less, take in everyone and specifically focus on the people we know. More often than not I don't even notice that someone I know is in the room…or saying hi… or waving.

I'm introverted, not anti-social.

The kind of aware I'm talking about makes me self-conscious about the space I take up in a room. I hear a constant echo of childhood commands to "Watch where you're going" and "Pay attention." And the result? I shrink. I assume there isn't space for me, that other people deserve to be where I was going to be, and that no one will want to hear from me anyway.

- When I fly, my seatmates always get the armrest. Or both seatmates if I'm in the middle. Because I'll move my arms—every time, without fail. I've even been known to voluntarily take the middle seat to make someone else more comfortable.

- When I'm in a crowd, I'll go out of my way to make sure I don't run into you. And if we do happen to bump purses, I'll apologize immediately.

- When I wait in the checkout line at Target, I put a self-imposed amount of space between your order and mine to give you the privacy you need to check out, so you don't feel rushed and so my items don't crowd yours.

- When I'm at Zumba I won't go into your space, take your spot, or dance too "big."

Of course, some of those examples toe the line between good manners and overkill, and I'm okay with the parts of my God-given personality that allow me to consider the needs of others. But as I've thought about what it looks like to live a life of holy hustle, I've watched some people I admire for their confidence, to see what they do differently.

They wake up early, but I do that too. I have a six-year-old. They make time to work out. It happens less often than I'd like, but I do that too. They drink enough water. Most of mine is used to make coffee, but that's close enough. They invest in personal development, and I love a good Bible study, a conference, and a John Maxwell quote, so I feel good about that one.

The factor that made these people stand out? I was struck by how they take up space. They stand with their feet wider, they move bigger, and they claim the space God has put them in without apology.

Maybe that's part of the lesson God wants to teach me through holy hustle. Because more than 30 years of making myself small and insignificant under the guise of good manners and humility has become exhausting.

When we have confidence in the call God has placed on our lives, it changes not just the way we take up physical space, but how we claim space in other ways for God's kingdom. What about the space prayer takes up in our lives? A friend shared with me recently that her interaction with God had grown slowly and subtly smaller as a reaction to the negative and discouraging responses of a friend. She used to dive into Scripture, seek God's will before meetings, pray boldly, and share with enthusiasm what God was doing in her life on social media. All it took to plant a seed of doubt that maybe she was taking up too much space with her enthusiasm and making others feel too uncomfortable were a few comments from a friend. And so until she could identify the toxic relationship and remove that doubt from her life, she withdrew.

My version of that story ended the same way but started in a different place. I worked with one of those larger-than-life personalities, the kind who fill a room with their presence and make themselves known as soon as they walk in the door. They never seem to be at a loss for words, always tell the perfect story for just the right occasion, have the most amazingly faith-filled prayer for every circumstance, and are always invited to speak, share, and do the big "famous" things. For someone like me who struggles to take up the space God has given me, that personality wasn't encouraging to my heart. It felt like a shadow I could never escape, an expectation I could never achieve. The result? I stopped praying at meetings because I knew my words would be ordinary and basic in comparison. I ceased sharing ideas because I wasn't the loudest voice in the room and it was better to choose to be quiet than to risk being skipped over and ignored—again. I stopped opening up to my coworkers because my stories weren't perfectly polished, funny, or charming.

My relationship with God grew quiet because I'd forgotten He isn't limited in His resources. I subconsciously lived as though keeping my small prayers quiet would free God up to deal with the bigger, more important prayers. If He didn't have to waste time listening to me, He could take care of the things He wanted to care for.

Unlike the people we'll interact with on a daily basis who, with the best intentions, have preferences and play favorites, God is limitless. I can't take up His time any more than you can. He wants to hear from each of us, no matter how big or small or silly or serious our prayer is. He makes space for us and calls us significant because we are His. We don't have to apologize for bothering Him or worry that we shouldn't be there. We don't have to wait for an invitation or perfect timing, and we're never standing too close or getting in the way.

I don't know if I'll be able to quiet those voices in my head in the line at Target, but I'm going to lean into the truth that God doesn't think I'm bothersome.

God has given us a specific space for a specific season. Let's claim it confidently, kindly, and unapologetically. Right here is where He has called us to work for His glory, and whatever the cost—no matter how inconvenient it is, embarrassing it is, or uncomfortable it might make us—occupying that space is worth it.

Jill Briscoe said, "You go where you're sent, and you stay where you're put, and you give what you've got until you're done."[1] When I first heard these words, they felt like freedom. It was as though I was granted release from the chains of fame, platform, and success that bound so many of us in that "next generation of women" as we observe the space others take up on their journeys.

◇◇◇◇◇

I'd like to introduce you to Ms. Jean. She lives in my same small town in a house that bumps up next to our local intermediate school. The laughter of fourth and fifth graders travels through her backyard, lingering in the garden she has so lovingly tended. I remember noticing her for the first time at church as she and her husband participated in the annual Christmas cantata. Their faces were filled with pure joy as they shared about Christ's birth through song.

Years later I found myself working with her son at our local bank, joining Ms. Jean for her monthly "mugs and muffins" Bible study, and after Madison was born, gathering in their home with other parents to learn how to raise children to love Jesus.

Ms. Jean is the kind of Bible teacher who pulls you into Scripture immediately and keeps you there until God has a chance to do a good work in your heart. It was never about her, and she was always the first to admit that public speaking wasn't a gift she felt came naturally. But she was obedient where God had called her, so she opened her home and her garden to anyone who needed a safe place to land.

Above their garage, Ms. Jean and her husband intentionally created a guesthouse that anyone could use at any time. There were only a couple of conditions—you couldn't pay them anything when you stayed there and it was a kid-free zone. They also had no television or internet. It was a retreat in the truest sense of the word, overlooking a secret garden in the middle of our town. NFL players and famous Christian speakers had stayed there, while local couples and missionaries who needed respite received the same warm welcome. God called Ms. Jean to serve Him through her generous hospitality and love for teaching, and she did—blooming right where she had been planted.

What would happen if, like Ms. Jean, we chose faith instead of striving for fame? Throughout Scripture God shows us that His Hall of

Faith (Hebrews 11) isn't made up of perfect, award-winning men and women. These were everyday people who trusted that where they were called was significant for the kingdom because God placed them there.

You aren't enough to do the holy hustle work God has set before you, but your small obedience is enough. Your gifts and your everyday, busy, imperfect, messy moments are full of opportunities to serve instead of striving. We have a greater impact on eternity when we go where we've been called, working together in community to create something beautiful for God's kingdom, and we stay there, giving it all we've got until the work is done.

<><><><>

We kicked soccer balls around the yard Sunday afternoon. It was warm, and the sun was shining, a taste of spring that felt a long time coming. No phones were out to take photos; nothing was needed to entertain us except one another. We played, and it filled my heart as much as it made our girl laugh.

The experience got the only two "likes" I needed—from my husband and daughter. They liked it because we were making memories together. The only hearts that were part of our time together were the happy ones the three of us had that warm winter Sunday.

It's easy to determine the worthiness of an experience by the response we receive online. Two likes and three hearts pale in comparison to the hundreds and thousands we see popping up on the accounts of the famous friends we follow. If my family's time together were displayed as a post on Instagram, I might be tempted to delete it, replace it with something else. I might reconsider what time I posted it, maybe adjust when and what I shared to get the memory in front of the most people.

As God calls me closer to Himself, He's revealing a version of hustle that looks a lot less impressive than the version I'd imagined. Leaning into a right-here faith means choosing the small moments over the popular ones because of the legacy it will leave for God's kingdom.

Holy hustle means standing firm and taking
up the space God has called you to, choosing a
life of faith, even if it never brings fame.

I was recently asked what I love to write about, and I stumbled around for a bit. As we talked, my friend picked up on something I said that I didn't even hear myself say, and she identified it as "my thing." She saw in me a calling to teach and encourage women to work hard and rest well, using their holy hustle for God's glory. And she spotted the joy in my voice when I talked about women working together— not against one another.

As someone who has been fired from a career she loved and asked to resign from a ministry she adored, I'd become blind to the gifts God had given me. The cost of growing in those gifts meant failing at what the world said I should be doing, at the titles it said I should have, and at the long hours I thought I should be working to support my family. Striving instead of serving had cost me my confidence, and as I shrank back from the places God was calling me, I failed to use the skills I'd been given. Until a friend spoke it to me, I couldn't see how God was making space in my life so I could claim the space into which He called me.

The talents and passions God built in me before I was even born? They've never shown up in my life as a fad. Unlike with my attempts to be a DIY blogger or to adopt a more popular writing style, these are the passions and skills that have come up again and again and again.

- A love of words.

- A love of God.

- A desire to see the internet used for God's kingdom.

- A belief that blogging and social media can be a mission field.

- A love of affirmation and encouragement.

- An ability to pick up the latest technology, apps, and trends with ease.

- An eye for design and love for learning.
- A heart to teach what I've been freely taught.

What is it for you? In a few minutes, we'll get to an exercise that will help you make that discovery.

Holy hustle means a small obedience with our gifts and a willingness to work with others can make a significant impact in God's kingdom.

Ephesians 4:1-3 (MSG) says it like this:

> I want you to get out there and walk—better yet, run!—on the road God called you to travel. I don't want any of you sitting around on your hands. I don't want anyone strolling off, down some path that goes nowhere. And mark that you do this with humility and discipline—not in fits and starts, but steadily, pouring yourselves out for each other in acts of love, alert at noticing differences and quick at mending fences.

That is a work-hard, rest-well lifestyle! No sitting around on your hands, binge watching television, or wishing you had her job or her life or her platform. Those are paths that go nowhere, and no matter how much space you take up, if God hasn't called you there, you won't fit in there. You'll wear yourself out trying to keep up when you could be pouring out your gifts in a way that loves your neighbors well—right where you are. When we stop running someone else's race, we can confidently take up the space God has given us, using our gifts for His glory.

What would you do differently if you could live in the freedom that comes from claiming your own lane? Would you change the kind of work you do or at least your attitude about your work? Would you be able to let go of past hurts and the labels you've carried for too long, stuck to you like so many HELLO, MY NAME IS name tags?

My inability to reconcile who God made me to be with the labels the world puts on my generation makes sense—because this isn't our home, and we aren't meant to fit in here. How thankful I am to now know we aren't bound by the titles, expectations, labels, or stereotypes of the world. When God calls us His children, He gives us new titles and a new way of living. No strolling around, sitting on our hands, waiting for someone else to do the work for us—or working ourselves to exhaustion, never taking a vacation, and missing time with our families. God has called us all to work hard and rest well, following His model and the examples He's given us throughout Scripture.

◇◇◇◇◇

So far we've looked at where God has called us, embraced the idea that small is effective, and thought about the areas God is asking us to use our gifts for His kingdom. But that last one can be hard. Finding my "thing" has taken years, not a few chapters of a book or a few days of thinking encouraging thoughts. And as long as it's taken me to figure out my unique set of gifts and God's version of holy hustle, it's taken me even longer to be okay with the voice God has given me and where He has me.

I'm not typically a "three easy steps!" kind of writer, but this is an exercise I've used with women that gives them an opportunity to focus on the gifts God has given them. It helps them consider how they can serve well, whether they're called to the quiet ministry of open-door hospitality, to an online platform, or to a large stage.

1. Write It Down—Grab your journal or notebook, a pen, and a your favorite comforting drink. Flip to an empty page and start writing down everything you love to do. Forget about what "she" does or what you think sounds impressive. What have you always done well? What did you want to be when you were little that still makes you excited when you think about it? What would you do if

money and time weren't obstacles? If tomorrow was your opportunity to do something with your talents, what would you do? Write until you run out of room, and then flip to a new page and keep writing. Look for themes, and cross out anything you wrote down because you thought you *should*, not because it's *you*.

2. Pray About It—Take a sip of your drink and push your notebook or journal away. Then spend time in prayer, thanking God for the gifts and talents He has given you. Ask Him to bring to light anything you might have forgotten. Be willing to cross off anything He makes it clear He doesn't intend for you to pursue in this season, and above all, choose His will over your comfort. Sometimes we must stop doing what we've always done and be willing to do what we've never done before to find our "thing."

3. Ask Others—Once you've spent time thinking through this on your own, and after you've prayed over your list, ask a few trusted, close friends for their opinion. This isn't the time to do an online survey or ask a few hundred acquaintances on Facebook what they think you do well. Seek out a handful of friends or family who are *for* you, who *know* you and your heart, and ask them what they think your "thing" is. In what areas do they consider you an expert? Ask them what task seems hard for them yet simple for you? Then review how their thoughts line up with your list.

These three steps seem so easy, but I know how hard they can be. Now is the time to silence the negative self-talk and lean into the place God has called you. Forget about measuring your gifts against the expectations of the world, and instead focus on the encouragement found in Scripture: "Do not despise these small beginnings, for the LORD rejoices to see the work begin" (Zechariah 4:10 NLT). That verse doesn't say the Lord rejoices to see your business card with your impressive title. It doesn't say He rejoices only when your God-sized dream comes true, or when you finally "make it." The Lord rejoices to see the work begin.

Often the cost of claiming the space God has called us to is the humbling of our hearts. When Scripture tells us just starting is enough, do you believe it? Can you do your very best work, even if you never see the fruit of your labor on this side of heaven? Ms. Jean could have stopped leading Bible study in her home years ago because she wasn't seeing the work God was doing in the hearts of the women who attended. She could have become discouraged when a small handful showed up instead of the dozens she was expecting. She could have created that guest space but kept it to herself, unable to see the worth of her work in keeping it clean and ready for guests who never gave her anything in return except their company.

I don't know about anyone else who had the pleasure of spending time with Ms. Jean, but I know this: her legacy of love, hospitality, service, and humility will live on in my life and be passed along to my daughter. Where Ms. Jean was faithful to start the work, God has been faithful to complete it. Philippians 1:6 (MSG) reminds us of this very promise: "There has never been the slightest doubt in my mind that the God who started this great work in you would keep at it and bring it to a flourishing finish on the very day Christ Jesus appears."

What you begin in faith, God will finish with a flourish.

◇◇◇◇◇

It was the aftermath of Christmas chaos, presents having been opened joyfully and played with for hours. No more fanfare, no more celebration, no more showing off the latest treasure to the newest guest. But Legos were all over our house. As the new year began, they became part of our daily life. I have a feeling these Legos are going to keep me on my toes, or at least wearing comfortable slippers as I try to step around them and not on them.

The larger Lego pieces are used first, of course. They're the ones that set the stage, the ones that overshadow the hundred little plastic bags full of nearly invisible parts, necessary and perfectly equipped for their purpose.

Sometimes I want nothing more than to be like those larger Legos pieces, the established, obvious choice. But the larger and more impressive Lego pieces don't make as much difference once the building is finished, not like you might think they would. As I picked up horses and mini figures, tiny hedgehogs, and sparkly snowflakes, I realized sometimes the smallest piece of the set makes the biggest impact.

- Little pieces of clear plastic, nearly invisible, create beautiful windows.

- Sparkly little dots add final touches to roofs and tables.

- Carrot noses complete snowmen, and tiny ice skates adorn tiny feet.

Often, I'm the accent piece that plays a small supporting role. The quiet one overshadowed by the larger-than-life personality. The one who assumes I'm easily replaceable or unnecessary for the finished product—nice to have, but not a "must have." But how generous of God to create the body of Christ specifically and intentionally to need every part—no matter how large or small.

> For as the body is one and has many parts, and all the parts of that body, though many, are one body—so also is Christ. For we were all baptized by one Spirit into one body—whether Jews or Greeks, whether slaves or free— and we were all made to drink of one Spirit. So the body is not one part but many (1 Corinthians 12:12-14).

Do you feel like one of the tiny, overlooked pieces in the kit? Are you still not sure that what looks plain and ordinary and messy could ever be part of the holy kingdom work your heart longs to offer to the world? Do you wonder how you can stay where God has called you when you aren't sure the work you've been given is good enough?

Have you looked at your list of things you love to do, talents you have, gifts you received, and still assumed plenty of others could do more, do it better, do it more impressively and stand out more? Lean in. God doesn't make mistakes when He places us, and He knows exactly what kind of special touch we'll add to His finished product. Your presence and your purpose matter. Whether we're the most impressive piece in a pile (helping others to stand firm!) or the smallest accent (shining brightly!), we glorify God when we unite for His kingdom.

You are irreplaceable, perfectly equipped, and incredibly necessary to the work God has planned for you. In Christ, we can do more than we could ever imagine.

Digging Deeper

It's one thing to write about claiming the space God has given us, staying where we've been placed until the work is done, and choosing right-here faith instead of fame. But how do we remain encouraged and motivated in our work when our social media friends and followers' lives look as if they've been sprinkled with MiracleGro while we sit hoping for a small ray of sunshine?

Earlier we read a verse from the book of Zechariah—"Do not despise these small beginnings, for the LORD rejoices to see the work begin" (4:10 NLT)—which I think can help us feel grounded and secure. But let's look at the whole story first, okay? My Bible shares this background: "Zechariah prophesied to a group of discouraged Israelites, announcing that it was a new day for God's chosen people. He sought to inspire those who had returned from captivity to rebuild the temple and rededicate their lives to the Lord."[2]

Maybe you're feeling discouraged today, not sure if the work you do matters. Maybe you're wondering if anyone notices, or if God still has work for you to do. Or you might be at the end of a particularly busy season, wondering if God has anything new for you. Oh, He does. God's message to those discouraged, worn-out Israelites can be a source of encouragement for our hearts today.

When these words were spoken to the Israelites, they had just come out of a season of terrible hardship. Their homes had been destroyed by invading armies, people had been killed, buildings had been demolished, and they had watched friends, family, and neighbors captured as slaves to foreign lands. Upon their return, they started to rebuild their beloved city. They got to work—until they ran into obstacles and the work stopped. Although daily life continued, everything around them "continued to lie in ruin for two more decades."[3]

Zechariah steps in to offer encouragement, not only to continue the work God had given the Israelites but for the people to rebuild their hearts and return to a relationship with God.

---

*When our hearts are in ruins, no work of our
hands will be useful for God's kingdom.*

I'll be the first to admit that this book of the Bible isn't the easiest to understand. It's full of poetic and complicated language, imagery, and visions from angels. But I think we might all be able to relate to this summary of chapter 4, verses 1-10: "Faced with rebuilding their temple and city, the chosen people felt small, powerless, and overwhelmed...But Zechariah saw things differently. God would empower the people."[4]

If the work God has called you to feels too large and overwhelming to do on your own, it's because God intends to fill our weaknesses with His strength. Holy hustle means more than just working hard and resting well. It's learning to trust God through the small beginnings, the unseen work, the overwhelming days, and the finished product—giving Him credit and glory, every step of the way.

As we look to the work God is giving us right now, right here, may we say yes to a right-here faith that says yes to work done "not by strength or by might, but by [God's] Spirit" (Zechariah 4:6).

Holy Hustle Story

JENNIFER: JOURNALIST

I have always been a girl who hustles. I knew it for sure the other day when I found my old high school letter jacket in the closet. Sure enough, it was covered with letters to mark my hard work in golf, basketball, track, drama, National Honor Society, band, vocal, and cheerleading. Whew! It wears me out just thinking about all the stuff that one kid tackled in four years! But honestly, it never felt like a burden. It felt like I was in my sweet spot of giving my all and doing my best. As I've grown older, I've carried that same trait of hustle with me. And I've learned how that can be a blessing—and a curse.

I'm in my sweet spot when I'm doing the work God created me to do, and doing it well. But I've also learned that I can overdo my doing. There's a distinction between hustle and over-hustle. When I'm hustling, I'm doing what I'm created to do in this world, to the best of my ability. When I'm over-hustling, I'm out of balance, out of whack, and probably out of God's will for my life. I have to guard against workaholism, perfectionism, and saying yes to everyone and everything.

Holy hustle, for me, means consciously working alongside God, happily doing what I was created to do to make the world a better place. I've learned that I can maximize my sweet spot by praying before doing my tasks and inviting Jesus into the work I'm doing while folding the laundry, balancing the books, pulling weeds, hiring a new employee, sweeping crumbs, or making copies. When I start to feel myself heading toward striving or wondering if the work I do matters, I remember John 5:17 (NCV), where Jesus said, "My Father never stops working, and so I keep working, too."

Reflection

Do you remember how I invited you to stand up and stretch when we first started this section? Let's do it again. This time, close your eyes. Stand up and move your feet just a little further apart. Stretch your arms up just a little higher. Tilt your chin up just a bit more than the first time. Roll those shoulders back and breathe deeply. God has called you to this particular place, for this specific season, and you can stand firm in the calling He has placed on your life.

Take a minute to reflect on the space God has called you into with your family, your neighbors, your coworkers, or your friends. Where have you missed an opportunity for small-moment obedience because you were striving for more? How can you serve more and strive less in those spaces this week?

God is in the business of expanding our small offerings into great riches for His kingdom. How can you begin your holy hustle work this week, no matter how small the first step?

What space has God called you to that you've been shying away from because you don't feel "good enough" to be there? What would you do differently if you believed God started a good work in you, He isn't done with you yet, and you aren't enough—but He will give you what you need?

Have you ever felt like the small, insignificant piece of the puzzle, sure no one would miss you if you weren't there? How has God been nudging your heart, affirming your gifts, encouraging your dreams, and using you in those small, ordinary, faith-filled and fame-free moments?

◇◇◇◇◇

"Hello, Hustle"

Gardens are not made by singing
"Oh, how beautiful!" and sitting in the shade.
RUDYARD KIPLING

'm a rule follower, not a risk taker. When my third-grade teacher told us the "desk fairy" would randomly check our desks at night after we'd gone home and distribute rewards to students who had clean, organized materials, I was all in. But when our gym teacher pulled out the dreaded tumbling mats, I would hang back, waiting for the rest of my classmates to somersault and cartwheel before I took my own, timid turn, too afraid of failing to truly learn the moves.

As an adult, I still find myself avoiding opportunities and experiences that don't have a guaranteed outcome. I was sure I would be a terrible mother and never had dreams about having children of my own—until my niece was born. Watching my twin sister with her beautiful little girl gave me the courage to open my heart to motherhood, even though I knew there was no way to organize, read, or prepare my way into success.

Fear can keep us from embracing the abundant life God desires for His children. Not the kind of abundance that gives us bigger bank accounts or a fully stocked cart at Target, but the kind of abundance that comes from living fully in the passions and place God has chosen for us.

As you prepare to say "hello" to hustle, what are you afraid of right now?

In the years God has allowed me to work online, with words and in ministry, I've learned something: when someone else is brave enough to go first, it gives us the courage to take our turn. I'll share some of my fears and anxieties about work, worth, hustle, and rest to get us started.

- I'm afraid that embracing hustle will mean saying good-bye to relaxation.

- I'm worried that I'll use hustle as an excuse to work all the time, blaming God for my busyness.

- I wonder if I've been saying yes to rest too often and will discover that I've become lazy.

- I feel anxious about what it will mean if none of this applies to the work God has called me to do.

- I'm sure this is a great message for someone else, but my work is too small to matter.

Isaiah 43:19 says, "Look, I am about to do something new; even now it is coming. Do you not see it? Indeed, I will make a way in the wilderness, rivers in the desert." We are created in the image of a God who does new things! God didn't design the world and then decide to sit back and watch it all unfold. He is still at work, doing new things in our lives, in our hearts, and through our work.

For a few decades, a group of women at our church called Secret Sisters has met monthly to encourage one another through fellowship and the exchange of gifts. Despite the group's name, their community is not secret. It's open to women of all ages and stages of life, from great-grandmothers to teen daughters. Recently they decided to do something new, to go down a new path that made friendship a longer lasting and more intentional part of their gathering. So they invited me to share my story and some encouragement at a recent meeting.

It was the first time I'd ever spoken to a group at a local chain restaurant, and the venue was unique, to say the least. As I followed the restaurant host past the stocked salad bar and the overflowing dinner buffet, I wondered how I would ever make my soft-spoken voice reach these women over the loud country music pumping through the ceiling speakers. Although the group leader and I had chatted recently on Facebook, we had never met in person, so I did some quick internet stalking in the parking lot to make sure I was going to introduce myself to the correct woman.

The private banquet room was lovely, but the walls stopped short of the ceiling by about four feet. The doorways were wide, generously designed to allow servers to pass through with trays of food with ease, but there were no doors to close. The bathrooms were close by, inviting all restaurant traffic to conveniently pass us on the other side of a short, thin wall. The ice machine rattled and hissed at the back of the room.

I could have been anxious, but I trusted that God could do a new thing regardless of the setup or the scenery. In my striving, I would have set myself up for disappointment. I would have imagined a perfect setting, more women, rapt attention. Instead, I prayed myself out of the way and asked God to allow them to forget most of what I said but to remember *all* of what He wanted to speak to their group.

By His grace the ice machine settled down and my voice carried far enough to reach the ladies several tables away. I shared handouts and small gifts, and we laughed together as restaurant staff stole looks into the room. Where I would have expected perfection, God asked for obedience, and when I decided to stop striving, He got to work. We talked a lot about Isaiah 43:19, how God doesn't tell us that He expects us to go and do a new thing or make a way in the wilderness while He watches from the sidelines. Our job is to trust that God is going to do a new thing and to look for it, expectantly.

Holy hustle means understanding the part of the work we're responsible for and stepping out of the way to let God do His part.

Adopting a new attitude and outlook about hustle takes time. But when it comes to change and the new things God wants to do in our lives, we have two choices: retreat or pursue growth. I'm the first to admit that sometimes retreat sounds better until God shows me my motivation. When change feels scary, it's because I'm relying on my strength to make it through. I assume it's all up to me to make it work, to make sure it succeeds, to make sure I don't look like a failure—again. When I choose to retreat it's because I'm being reminded that on my own, in my striving, I won't be able to make it all work out the way I want it to.

But then I stop striving and start pursuing, trusting that God is bringing a new thing because He has plans for me that are good, plans that will bring Him glory and expand His kingdom.

Will you lean into the new path He's leading you on, one where holy hustle replaces striving? Or will you retreat, preferring the comfort of what is known to an uncomfortable season full of unknowns?

Here are three assurances we can take confidently into the future: God is not done with us yet, He's ready to do a new thing, and He is there with us every step of the way.

◇◇◇◇◇

Ecclesiastes 9:10 is a Scripture I've found incredibly encouraging in those seasons when I wondered if any of my work made a difference, or if I should be working harder or doing more. It says, "Whatever your hands find to do, do with all your strength." Striving tells us we should do everything with all our might. Striving is the voice that tells us we aren't good enough, that makes us doubt ourselves and our passions as we scroll through Instagram or Pinterest. Striving is the nagging voice that says our meager efforts will create the results we want, that the only way to land that promotion, ministry position, dream job, tidy house, or Pinterest-perfect family is to work hard at everything, all the time. We sign up for more courses, read more books, join more groups in real life and on Facebook, and we have a never-ending to-do list with ideas that will surely get us noticed.

Holy hustle gives us the freedom to work hard with all our might on the tasks God assigns to our soul. This is the heart work, the work that makes a difference in God's kingdom. Holy hustle gives us the freedom to recognize that the work others do is right for them, but not for us, not in this season. Holy hustle helps us to hear God over the roar of the bossy world, so we can say yes to the work God has prepared our hearts for and no to the work that will drain our souls.

When we live in the freedom of holy hustle, we can rest knowing that God's no just means not yet, not never.

The line between hustle and striving, rest and laziness, is a delicate place to live. When we lean too far one way, we find ourselves relying on our strength instead of abiding in God's reminders that He is our strength.

- The LORD is my strength and my song; He has become my salvation. (Exodus 15:2)

- The LORD is my strength and my shield; my heart trusts in Him, and I am helped. (Psalm 28:7)

- My God is my strength. (Isaiah 49:5)

- Yahweh my Lord is my strength; He makes my feet like those of a deer and enables me to walk on mountain heights! (Habakkuk 3:19)

But how do we know which side of the line we fall on? And when we figure out where we are on the scale of striving, holy hustle, and laziness, how do we course correct to get back in line with God's will for our work? Let's go through a few quick questions to see where we land, and then together we'll discover how to take steps to move closer to the place God wants us to be.

For each question below, choose A, B, or C, based on what you would typically do on a standard day.

1. When given a task to complete, do you:

   a. Assume no one else will do the work, and it's up to you to get it done?

   b. Talk to your team to see who has the right gifts to do the job well?

   c. Feel overwhelmed and avoid eye contact until someone else starts the work?

2. When it comes to your position or reputation, do you:

   a. Often feel like you need to fight and prove yourself by doing more?

   b. Trust that God has you here for a reason and rest knowing He will fight for you?

   c. Do the bare minimum required and then are surprised when others receive recognition or rewards instead of you?

3. Around the dinner table, does your family:

   a. Ask you why you're so stressed/upset all the time?

   b. Appreciate the boundaries you've put on your work so you can join them?

   c. Feel stress because they've been working hard while you've been relaxing—again?

4. You have a goal in mind. Will you:

   a. Do what it takes to get there, even if it means taking a break from hobbies, friendships, or time with family?

   b. Work toward it as time/resources allow but remain intentional about resting?

   c. Do nothing, assuming you'll probably fail anyway?

5. When your plans for the day don't go the way you hoped, do you:

    a. Rush around trying to make it work anyway, feeling annoyed?

    b. Stay flexible, not frustrated?

    c. Shrug and let someone else deal with it?

6. When you look at your to-do list at the end of the day, do you:

    a. Feel like you need to do more to prove your worth?

    b. Feel peaceful about the amount of work you've done?

    c. Realize you were so overwhelmed by all that needed to be done that you did nothing?

7. After a day of rest, do you feel:

    a. Stressed?

    b. Refreshed?

    c. Tired and worn-out?

8. Your home, work, and personal life are in disarray. Do you:

    a. Work tirelessly to fix it all on your own?

    b. Prioritize the work and spend time in prayer, asking God to heal and fix the things that are out of your control?

    c. Choose to binge watch a show to avoid the emotional work required to deal with it all?

Look at your responses.

- If you chose mostly A answers, you might find yourself on the striving side of the scale.

- If you chose mostly B, you have likely found yourself in the sweet spot of holy hustle.
- If you chose mostly C, you might find yourself on the lazy rest side of the scale.

We will all float along this scale throughout our lives, finding ourselves leaning too far into a season of laziness disguised as rest, or too far into a season of striving instead of serving. This scale isn't meant to be a permanent description of our lives, but a tool to keep our hearts in check so we can take the necessary steps to slide back into the middle, where God asks us to both work hard *and* rest well.

If you found yourself on the striving side of the scale today, take some time right now to write down all the jobs you're doing. Spend time thinking about and praying over that list, asking God to reveal your motivations. What *are* your real motivations behind the goals you've set for yourself and the items on that to-do list? Who is getting the glory through that work? Where are you ignoring the nudges of God to say no to something good so He can make room for something great? Where are you afraid you'll miss out on something important if you don't participate/attend/impress?

Write down anything God reveals to your heart and make a conscious decision to lay your agenda at the foot of the cross every morning, waiting on what God wants you to do that day. Grab a Post-it note and write down Luke 18:7 from *The Message* to remind you that you don't need to be the one who fights—God will take care of you. "Won't he stick up for them? I assure you, he will. He will not drag his feet."

Maybe you found yourself pretty far over on the rest side of the scale today. Rest, grace, and soul-care are all good things. Our hearts need time to refill from the emotional exertion of the week. Our minds need rest and respite from the intellectual efforts of our days. And our souls need time and space to reconnect with God so we can hear His still, small voice over the bossy demands of the world. But when we stay in those seasons of rest beyond the refueling our bodies, minds, and hearts need, we become less effective for God's kingdom.

Think of it this way: When you work out, your body is being

pushed to its maximum to allow the muscle fibers to break down. You reach a period of fatigue when your muscles fail because you've done all the work you can do, and now they need to recover. As your muscles rest and you fuel your body with the right kinds of food, those fatigued muscle fibers are rebuilt—now stronger than they were before. If instead you skip the hard work entirely and stop using those muscles, they atrophy. You become weak, and simple tasks become a struggle. Your body requires a balance of work and rest to give it strength.

When you think about the tasks God has given you to do, have an honest conversation with yourself. Have you been neglecting them? Have you chosen an extended season of rest that has allowed your spiritual muscles to atrophy? Are the activities you're choosing to do when you rest filling you with joy and energy, or do you feel even more tired than when you started? Write down where God is revealing that you've taken rest a little too far, and ask Him where He wants you to start using your gifts again. Write Psalm 18:1 from *The Message* on a Post-it note to remind you that the work we're called to isn't meant to be done in our strength: "I love you, GOD—you make me strong."

For those of you who found yourself hovering beautifully near that sweet spot in the middle, where working hard and resting well meet? Welcome to holy hustle. This is the place God designed for us with His example of work at the very beginning of time. With God's agenda in charge and our to-do lists given over to His will, we get to work. Interruptions in our days aren't meant to be frustrating, but are instead invitations to watch with anticipation for the new things God is going to do in our day. When we prioritize people over programs, God's glory over our success, and choose faith instead of fame, we can release the guilt of working hard and say good-bye to the shame of resting well.

In this space, we can make an impact on our families, our friends, our communities, and our coworkers because we are at our peak spiritual and physical condition. With each day of hard work, we grow stronger in obedience, love, compassion, encouragement, self-control, and faith. With each day of resting well, we refuel with the people, places, and activities that bring us refreshment and joy.

Take some time to thank God for the refining work He has done in your life. Acknowledge the areas where you may still find yourself sliding over into striving or laziness and ask Him to reveal any specific places you need to watch.

If you haven't given God the glory for a recent success or opportunity, do it now, praising Him for what He has done in your life and through your work. On another Post-it note, write Colossians 2:7 from *The Message* as a reminder to give thanks for all God has done to get you to this place: "Let your living spill over into thanksgiving."

Hopefully, you're starting to grasp how holy hustle is different from the kind of hustle we see in the world around us. This version of hustle means we're not ashamed to go hard after the things God is calling us to do or the place He has called us to do it. Instead of using others to get ourselves ahead, we commit to using the gifts and talents God has given us wisely and effectively. With holy hustle, we promote what God is doing in our lives, not ourselves. This version of hustle is not about finding more time in our day to do more, but discovering what God is calling us to do so we can serve more, give more, encourage more—in the right places and right ways.

Digging Deeper

This is where it all begins. The book of Genesis "unfolds God's original purpose for humanity."[1] From God's plan for us as His sons and daughters, our relationship with Him, with one another, and with creation to His example of work, God doesn't just create the world out of nothing and leave us to fend for ourselves. When I find myself striving and assuming I'm responsible for making sure everything gets done, I forget to rely on the only One who can do it all. I, like Eve, listen to the tempting voice of the world that draws me toward what looks good but isn't God's best for my life. I've taken a bite of that apple far more often than I care to admit.

I love that this is the very first sentence in the entire Bible: "In the beginning God created the heavens and the earth" (Genesis 1:1). It makes sense on a practical level that we would need to have some creation story to tell us where we came from and how it all happened. What I love, though, are these two words: "God created." It doesn't say "God commanded" or "God demanded" or "God bossed someone else around" or "God snapped His fingers." We are designed to reflect the image of a God who creates, and we do that through the work we do. Creating takes time and imagination, creativity and care. How would you view the work you do differently if you saw it through the lens of a new title: "child of God: creative"?

You can bring beauty and life to the work you've been given. Will you create life with the words you speak today, words laced with grace and kindness? Or will you make something amazing in the kitchen, feeding your family food that isn't just nourishing but made with love? We can take a page out of God's book and bring light to dark places, right where God has called us.

As we dig further into these opening verses of Genesis, we get a glimpse of the kind of work/rest balance God modeled for us. Just as Scripture gives us instruction on how to be a good friend and neighbor, how to honor God with our finances, and how to receive the gift of salvation, we can also apply God's vision for work to our lives.

> By the seventh day God completed His work that He
> had done, and He rested on the seventh day from all His
> work that He had done. God blessed the seventh day and
> declared it holy, for on it He rested from His work of
> creation (Genesis 2:2-3).

So often I've read through the creation story and focused on either the order God created everything or the interaction between Him and Adam and Eve. I knew God called work good, but had I ever noticed that He called rest "holy"? Good and holy. Work and rest. The same God who created everything out of nothing, who is infinitely more powerful than we could imagine, chose to rest. Why, then, do I find myself working nonstop, striving to do more and do it bigger and better than the next person? When I believe I'm too essential to my work to take the time to rest, I forget who gave me the work to do in the first place. And when I believe I deserve more rest and less work, I neglect the people God has asked me to serve.

God worked and created for six days. He did the work until it was done, and then He rested. How often do I do some of the work and call it "enough"? How often do I do more than what is asked or expected of me and find myself weary and burned-out? Matthew Henry's commentary on this section of Scripture reminds us that God didn't rest because He was weary, but because He had finished the work. Our weariness may be an indicator that we are living outside the holy hustle God modeled for us, striving instead of serving.

> The eternal God, though infinitely happy in the enjoyment of himself, yet took a satisfaction in the work of his own hands. He did not rest, as one weary, but as one well-pleased with the instances of his own goodness and the manifestations of his own glory.[2]

What if we were to live well pleased with the work we've done each day? Not looking around social media and wishing for more, or staring blankly at our to-do lists, wondering at the end of the day what happened, but pleased with the work God has allowed us to do, regardless of how small, insignificant, or outside of our agenda it was? As we pay attention to the little ways God invites us to be creative in our daily work, we might just find ourselves taking satisfaction in the work of our hands even when our location, circumstances, titles, and paychecks never change.

Although we'll spend an entire chapter talking about rest, let's take a quick look at what God designs for us on day seven of creation in Genesis 2. When all the work has been completed to God's satisfaction, and He has called it good, He doesn't start a new project or begin redesigning what He's already finished. He rests. My Bible commentary points out that "this is the only instance during the creation process when God blessed a unit of time. The term holy is applied in the Bible to something set aside for the service of God."[3]

Rest doesn't just happen when we crawl exhausted into our beds at night. This kind of rest, a sabbath from the work God has called us to, is a restorative time for our hearts to honor God. As Matthew Henry puts it, "The sabbath day is a blessed day, for God blessed it, and that which he blesses is blessed indeed. God has put an honor upon it, has appointed us, on that day, to bless him, and has promised, on that day, to meet us and bless us."[4]

We were designed to do work that honors God, and we were created to spend time abiding with the Father so He can meet us where we are and bless us. When we adopt the world's version of non-stop hustle, we miss the moments God is inviting us to pause, reconnect, and be blessed. Living in the sweet spot of holy hustle allows us to bring glory to God through our work *and* our rest.

Holy Hustle Story

BRI: HOME COOK

I've always been a hard worker. I'm extremely goal oriented and I *love* lists. I thrive on deadlines. But God has been consistent to remind me that we are co-laborers together. He will equip me to do the work He has laid before me, and then I can trust Him to show up and use that work in a way that will bring great glory to Himself, even if He uses it in an unexpected way.

To me, holy hustle is consistently pursuing the work God has given me with gratitude. I'm careful to allow the Holy Spirit to strip every obstacle that hinders and then to get out of the way and pause, allowing God to further His kingdom with my work as He sees fit. When I find myself living outside of that work/rest balance, I come back to Hebrews 12:1-3, which says:

> Therefore, since we also have such a large cloud of witnesses surrounding us, let us lay aside every weight and the sin that so easily ensnares us. Let us run with endurance the race that lies before us, keeping our eyes on Jesus, the source and perfecter of our faith, who for the joy that lay before Him endured a cross and despised the shame and has sat down at the right hand of God's throne.

Reflection

Now that we've explored where we currently fall on the work/rest scale, and we've looked at the beautifully simple way God has demonstrated His desire for this area of our lives, what do we do next? How do we, like Bri, begin to trust that God will show up and work alongside us, meeting us in our work and blessing our rest?

As you think about where you landed in the quiz earlier, what is one small thing you can commit to doing this week to help slide the balance a little closer to that sweet spot of holy hustle?

Where is God asking you to trust Him and allow the work you've done to be "good"—even if it doesn't feel finished?

How did our short discussion about Sabbath change how you view rest? What blessings do you think you've missed because you haven't embraced a God-honoring style of rest?

◇◇◇◇◇

_____

_____

_____

_____

_____

_____

_____

_____

_____

_____

_____

_____

5

Harvesting the Blessing

I would never want to reach out someday with a soft, uncallused hand—a hand never dirtied by serving—and shake the nail-pierced hand of Jesus.

BILL HYBELS

What if the work we were called to do was for more than personal gain—to receive God's blessings? As we dig further into this idea of holy hustle, we'll explore the Scripture God used to kick-start this journey for me as we go into the book of Ruth, and we'll look at the blessings that come when we hustle to do work that brings glory to God and not ourselves.

Sometimes God uses His Word to remind me that every piece of Scripture is relevant and able to work in my life, no matter the season or circumstances. This was one of those moments.

I'd read the book of Ruth before. I'd done whole Bible studies on this story. And yet when I most needed encouragement from God that there was worth in the work He had given me, this is where He brought me.

Ruth. That same Ruth who left her family, friends, and culture behind to follow her mother-in-law, Naomi, home to an unknown land. For so long that was the part of the story I focused on. How brave she was to do that! What courage, loyalty, and love Ruth must have had for Naomi! Her faith to say yes to a God she barely knew! In seasons of loneliness and broken community, Ruth's story brought me comfort as a fellow woman in a new, unknown land. This was a real-life fairy tale, and I loved how God redeemed her story, and I craved that for myself. I knew Jesus was my "Boaz"—the Redeemer who would come and rescue me.

Oh, but there is so much more to her story. As I listened to my pastor speak on this passage of Scripture one Sunday, I found myself reading ahead, skimming over the parts I already knew until God stopped me. After Ruth promised Naomi she would stay by her side, going where she was going, choosing to honor God as the only God, Ruth showed her determination to go to the fields and gather food for her family. Well aware of the customs, Ruth knew she'd be allowed to glean freely along the edges of a nearby field with permission. Here's my favorite part.

> Boaz asked his servant who was in charge of the harvesters, "Whose young woman is this?" The servant answered, "She is the young Moabite woman who returned with Naomi from the land of Moab. She asked, 'Will you let me gather fallen grain among the bundles behind the harvesters?' She came and has remained from early morning until now, except that she rested a little in the shelter" (Ruth 2:5-7).

Ruth didn't show up and do the bare minimum to get by. She hustled. She worked hard, respectfully, resting when needed, and finishing the work that was before her. The rest of the passage says she worked until evening, gathering 26 quarts of barley. Ruth showed up to work, and God worked out a plan through her life that would lead to her marriage to Boaz and her place in the lineage of Jesus.

By honoring God and serving her family, Ruth was blessed beyond anything she could have imagined.

That is holy hustle. Ruth wasn't motivated by popularity or recognition. Gathering grain was hard, back-breaking work. It wasn't fancy or famous or impressive. It was humbling. Ruth's work had meaning and purpose, and I believe ours does too.

When we work hard in the places God has called us to, faithfully and humbly serving Him, we can hustle without guilt or condemnation. It's holy hustle, and our work has worth in the kingdom of God.

What if Ruth had looked around the small home she shared with Naomi and focused more on what they lacked than on what she could provide? What if Ruth had gone out to seek work that would make her feel important instead of doing the work that would put her right where God wanted her? She may have missed the harvest entirely, as well as the blessings God wanted to give her as He redeemed her family.

When we strive to fix things on our own in big ways,
we miss the small gifts God has set in place for us.

It can be hard to go out and do the hard work God has called us to do. Maybe you've been asked to serve in a workplace that doesn't honor God, and you feel like the stranger in a foreign land. Or maybe God has brought you to a new place, and your dreams of doing impressive work that would bring recognition and fame have been replaced with a call to serve in a much smaller way. Maybe you've been serving faithfully in a role that you love but feel frustrated that you don't see the fruit of your work.

When we stop striving and start serving, we begin to trust God to harvest what we're faithfully planting. The kindness you bring to your workplace may be the very thing that draws someone closer to God. The love you show to others in the small, unseen, faithful places may be the very stepping-stone God will use to bring people closer to Himself. And those seeds you plant in faith may one day, generations after you've been gone from this earth, be the catalyst to a beautiful gift God wants to share with the world.

In those moments when I wonder if my work is worth the sometimes heartache and struggle, I remind myself that Ruth never went out to that field with the intention of becoming part of the ancestral line of Jesus. She saw a need for her family and worked faithfully, with kindness, right where she was until the work was done.

Maybe, like me, you're still a work-in-progress when it comes to developing a Ruth-like work ethic. I'll be the first to admit that one of the reasons I find myself striving is because I love control. I like to know what my day is going to look like, what to expect, and why it's worth my effort. When things don't go well, or I don't see an immediate result to the work I've done, it's easier to get frustrated and move on to the next item on my to-do list than to wait patiently and put my personal agenda aside.

But God is teaching me to trust Him, and He wants to do the same for you. He is faithful to show us that His plan for our lives isn't defined by how many items we can check off on our calendar each day, but by the small moments of obedience when we faithfully follow His call without needing to know "what's in it for me."

When it comes to striving, what would you identify as your biggest stumbling block—the one thing that keeps you from serving with a content spirit right where you are today? Maybe, like me, it's about control. Or maybe it's fear, insecurity, or something else. Identify it, write it down, and give it over to Jesus. Spend a few minutes in prayer, asking Him to free you from whatever is holding you back from living the full, content, obedient life He has designed for you and to help you remain alert in case those stumbling blocks show up again. Trust that God will not only use you where He's called you, but that He will use even the things that trip you up to move you further along in His plan.

God will take all the broken pieces of our lives that feel like failures and turn them into stepping-stones to guide us to the places He wants to take us next. As in a glass mosaic, each of those pieces on its own looks shattered and useless, but God will use each one to create something strong, beautiful, and purposeful.

Like Ruth, may we commit our lives to serving God to our utmost wherever He sends us, whether in motherhood, at McDonald's, or on a conference stage. Our holy hustle is not limited by our vocation or our location. Your gift of hospitality can be used to greet customers at your local bookstore. Your talent for finances can be used to serve your local PTO as a volunteer treasurer. The love you have for leadership can be used to honor God as a Bible study teacher, camp counselor, office manager, crossing guard, or stay-at-home mom. What field has God given you to work in, in this season? How can you serve and honor Him with your gifts?

When I devalue the gifts God has given me and assume they aren't enough, or that the place I've been called to use them is too small, I not only miss the blessings God has for me, but I rob others of the blessing of allowing God to harvest something beautiful from our shared experience.

As I learn to trust God and live in that space of right-here faith, I'm learning to appreciate the unexpected blessings of behind-the-scenes service. What if we all said yes to the edge of the field instead of fighting to run the show? Although incredibly talented men and women take center stage, encouraging and motivating and teaching from large platforms to thousands of people, who will say yes to serving the ones on the outside, the ones who can't make it to the arenas? What if we view our neighbors and communities, those right-here spaces where God has planted us, as our own harvest field? Could we be like Ruth, content to hustle on the fringes? What if:

- You used your love for hospitality to start a book club for your neighborhood?

- You served your church by volunteering to use your passion for social media to help promote an upcoming event?

- You said yes to sharing your testimony, even though it made you uncomfortable?

- You taught a free class for kids in your community to teach them about your talent?

- You volunteered at a local organization that needs your decorating and organizational skills?

- You showed up and served, simply because God said, "Go there"?

Saying good-bye to the fears and insecurities that hold us back makes room for God to pour into us His strength and courage.

In my current season of work as a freelance writer and communications consultant, I battle a daily stream of anxieties. My work isn't guaranteed, and it's certainly not easy. But I'm learning to trust God, and as I release control daily, my hands are open to receive His blessings. I must trust that He will take the words I write and use them to touch the hearts of people in a different state, giving them the motivation to use their gifts to serve kids in their communities who desperately need someone to stand up for them.

From my home office, there isn't much I can do to physically help kids in Texas who are in foster care, or who are courageously making life-changing decisions in residential treatment centers to change the future statistics tell them will happen. But I can share their stories. I can be faithful to do the work God is giving me to my absolute best. Because these are God's kids, the ones on the fringes who will never hear a famous speaker in a megachurch or attend a conference or a TED Talk.

But the words I put together might inspire someone to attend an event where they will have the opportunity to write words of encouragement and hope in a journal that *will* make it into the hands of one of these amazing kids. I don't need to know the outcome of the entire story to trust that—just as God knew at the end of His time designing creation—when my part of the work is done, it is good.

I used to believe the rewards that motivated me to do the tasks I'd been assigned were the kinds of things that could be shown off at networking events. I strove for those titles, impressive positions, and public recognition. Online personality tests tell me I'm adaptable, excelling, driven, introverted, responsible, image-conscious, and creative. Take a few minutes to consider your own personality traits, making a list of what you've learned from your own experiences with personality tests, what you view as your strengths, and what others say makes you stand out.

On paper, I'm the kind of person you want on your team when I'm living in that sweet spot of creativity and passion. But when we begin to slide outside of the healthy aspects of our personality type, driven becomes demanding and image-conscious becomes deceptive. Maybe you've experienced how your gift of organization can be overbearing, or your love for encouragement can result in envy as you spend so much time praising the accomplishments of others. At our best, we can be considered a role model who inspires. But when we start to let our fears of unworthiness run the show, we can manipulate "blessings" into existence without waiting on God because we need to not only be affirmed, but to be assured we have value.

When you trust that the God who built every aspect of your personality has plans for it that are good—not just for you, but for the people He asks you to serve—you can lay your fears at the foot of the cross and rest in that healthy space where you live fully in the abundant blessings of being His daughter. I wish I could tell you I've never experienced the negative, stress-filled, burned-out side of myself that happens when I allow myself to run the show. I have been quite present for every one of my sins and am aware that I have, more than once in the past, slid too far into "what's in it for me." If you find yourself striving for recognition, advancement, or opportunity and becoming apathetic or envious along the way, there's an easy solution: service.

God has given us all beautiful abilities and distinct personalities that can be used to honor others and, in return, receive the kind of blessings that last far longer than our careers. He will make our names great (Genesis 12:2) if it is part of His plan. We don't need to strive for fame. Far too often we find ourselves wishing for more, wanting the rewards and blessings we see others receiving for the same kind of work we're doing, and we forget to stop and thank God for what He's already given us. When we're constantly clamoring for more, we miss the smaller but more significant gifts God has in store.

Lara Casey says it this way in her book *Make It Happen*:

> If there is a "secret" to life it's this: following God is far more valuable than all the riches and comforts in the world. Whatever you are going through right now, if it's humbling you, making you pray, bringing you to your knees, and making you feel like you cannot do this alone, maybe there is a reason—a glorious, beautiful reason. Following Him

means taking giant leaps of faith, giving up your ways for *the* way, your life for *the* life, your truth for *the* truth. Following Him may mean leaving your job, or it may mean staying right where you are. It may mean hard work, choosing to go to uncharted territory, and diving headfirst into your fears, but He never fails, and He has a very good plan.[1]

Choose to harvest the blessings of holy hustle by putting aside what you think is best and lean into the blessings you never knew you needed. While we are focused on success, God wants us to focus on people. While we climb the corporate ladder, God wants us to offer a helping hand. While we find ourselves striving for more, God wants us to savor the lessons He wanted us to learn so we can grow to be more like Him.

Let's look for the blessings God has placed in our paths this week as we remain obedient to the work before us. Thank Him for the ways He has used failure as a stepping-stone to a new place. Go before God in thanksgiving for the people He has brought into your life because of the work you do. And remain aware, waiting with an expectant heart for the gifts He has yet to reveal. Plant the seeds in faith and trust God in the harvest.

Digging Deeper

Read Ruth 1–2

Although we worked through a bit of this story earlier, I want to make sure we dedicate some more time to exploring Ruth's holy hustle. I love that God would take the story of Naomi, forced to move to a foreign land because of famine, and redeem her family through a harvest. Naomi, it is assumed, left Bethlehem full of possessions and stature to avoid the emptiness of famine, but now she has returned empty of everything. Yet she will soon, through the obedience of Ruth and the kindness of Boaz, have her life filled and redeemed.

Unlike what we might find on a modern-day talk show, Naomi may have known she had wealthy relatives in the town, but instead of knocking on their door and demanding a handout, she and Ruth found a small home, expecting nothing of her neighbors or relatives. Through hard work their prayers would be answered and Ruth would experience the favor and blessing of a God she had only just accepted as her own. Matthew Henry's commentary points out that "God has chosen the poor of this world; and poor they are likely to be, for, though God has chosen them, commonly men overlook them."[2]

Ruth could have easily looked at their situation and decided to return home. She could have spent time wandering around town, trying to find a source of employment that would be impressive, putting her back to the standard of living she was accustomed to in Moab. She could have gone back to her parents and asked for assistance. Instead, she humbled herself and took on the hard, demanding job of gleaning in the fields because she had promised to be faithful to Naomi. They needed food, and she would do honorable, hard work to get it.

When life doesn't turn out the way you planned, what is your typical response? Think about the last time life felt unfair. Maybe you were fired from a job, didn't get the promotion you hoped for, received a hurtful rejection, or felt like part of a long-time dream had been crushed. Did you respond with acceptance or shame? Did you find yourself looking for someone to blame, or did you remain humble and hope to learn from the experience? We can look to Ruth as an example of how choosing the hard, narrow road of humility honors God, ourselves, and our families far more than allowing our pride to run the show. "She does not say, 'I will go and glean, and surely nobody will deny me the liberty,' but, 'I will go and glean, in the hope that somebody will allow me the liberty.'"[3]

God didn't place Ruth in just any old field. He directed her steps to *the* field that would make all the difference. Ruth didn't spend her time researching the fields and the men who ran them, interviewing other servants to find out which one was the best fit, spending a few hours at each to see which one met her needs the best. Ruth listened to Naomi's guidance and went to work, and God arranged the rest.

Ruth wasn't the only one who hustled that day. Boaz could have left the harvest in the capable hands of his team, spending his time doing what could have been seen as a more important or better use of his time. But he showed up in the field, distinctly aware of who was working, what they were doing, and whom he didn't recognize. Ruth humbled herself to serve her family while Boaz was humble enough to interact with his workers in a way that encouraged their respect.

When he tells his men to protect Ruth, there is no question of their obedience. When he asks them to bend the rules a bit and allow Ruth to glean from more choice areas of the harvest, there is no debate. While Ruth's reputation precedes her, Boaz's reputation exceeds her expectations. He goes beyond allowing her the liberty of a place with the servants and offers blessings beyond what Ruth or Naomi could have asked for or imagined.

Ruth was determined to do the work required to provide for her family, and although she rested and took time to eat what was provided, she didn't look at the favor she'd been given and leave to share the good news with Naomi.

She got back to work until the work was finished.

Ruth is a beautiful example of what it means to stay where God has called us until the work is done. She was in a new place, in a new job, with no experience and an unknown future. Rather than allow her circumstances to push her to strive and scramble and make a way for herself, Ruth saw a way to serve her family and did it with her whole heart through not just one harvest season, but two. From famine to harvest, from loneliness to redemption, God beautifully wove these two humble, hardworking children into the very tapestry of Jesus's lineage.

Holy Hustle Story

HAYLEY: BUSINESS OWNER

I've struggled with the idea of *hustle* forever. I had a mom who worked full, *full*-time when I was a kid. I missed being at home (I was always at day care) and I missed knowing my neighbors, having my mom being friends with the "other moms," and all that goes along with having a stay-at-home mom.

I've always wanted my kids to have quantity time with me as well as quality time, but it has become obvious that my husband and I are meant to work together. We complement one another and enjoy building things together. So as my ministry/work commitments grew, so did my responsibilities to those outside my house. That meant I couldn't just work at naptime anymore.

I have fought and fought this, but I've finally come to a peace about the idea that my kids are *fine*. They are the Lord's anyway. They are going to be disappointed in my parenting to some degree anyway. And, above all, I need to be obedient to the Lord and a full person while I'm here on the earth. My children are very important to me, but they are not everything. I think it's a privileged, wealthy American concept of Christianity to center everything on our kids, and, honestly, I think being a working *mom* is what brings the dismay, the guilt, the shame. I don't know that many people would feel bad being a working wife, or a working single.

The Lord has been slowly dragging me further and further out of my comfort zone and my plan, causing me to cling more tightly to Him and His plan. Holy hustle to me is not denying what God has called you to do, but working for His glory, in His time, and always in obedience.

When I need a gentle reminder, I focus on Galatians 5:1: "It is for freedom that Christ has set you free" (NIV). Mostly it reminds me that I put a lot of cultural constraints on myself when they're not of the Lord. I make sure when I feel the *I shoulds* creep in that I hold them up to the mirror of Scripture and take on the burden only if they're in there.

Reflection

Now that we've dug into Ruth's story a little more and have considered the blessings God wants to harvest through our obedience, can you think of some ways God has blessed your faithful, hard work? As you prepare to do the work God has called you to today, or this week, or in this season, how might your perspective change when you view your job like a farmer who plants seeds, patiently waiting for the right time for the harvest?

How does understanding your personality type help you approach a work/rest balance? Where might God be nudging you to make some healthier changes to get back to the place He created you to thrive in?

You, like Ruth, can make hard, humble decisions in your daily holy hustle. As we go forward from this point, having taken the time to explore what it means to work hard without shame, we'll begin to look outside of the blessings we receive when we model our work after God's example and explore what it means to serve others, collaborate instead of compete, and rest well without guilt. Unlike the world's view of hustle, the kind of hard work God calls us to happens best when we link arms with one another.

◇◇◇◇◇

_____

_____

_____

_____

_____

_____

_____

_____

The Superpower of Service

Success is...knowing your purpose in life, growing to reach your maximum potential, and sowing seeds that benefit others.

JOHN C. MAXWELL

flipped open a copy of John Ortberg's book *All the Places to Go... How Will You Know?* as I sipped on my perfectly warm nonfat caramel macchiato. The spring rain drizzled down the windows at Starbucks. After a season of work, friendship, and community loss, I didn't fully understand his question. "How will you know?" seemed to have a pretty obvious answer to me—I would say yes to anything that came my way because nothing was currently coming my way. Although I'd stopped striving as much to make opportunities happen in my own power, waiting on God was still something I found myself having to intentionally practice every day.

So I sat and I read Ortberg's book. I realized that in all my striving I had forgotten to have eyes open to the moments God was putting before me to serve. Ortberg calls them "doors" and says that "to be an open-door person means to embrace an open mind-set—along with a set of disciplines and practices to help us regularly embrace and walk through open doors."[1] Maybe it was the caffeine from that macchiato kicking in, or the sleepy fuzz finally drifting off my brain for the day, but it clicked. I'd spent more than ten years in such survival mode—as I graduated college, found a job to make ends meet, got married, functioned under the high-stress version of the world's definition of hustle, was fired, scrambled to find the next thing, started my own business, said yes to a ministry position that was intense and wonderful and lonely, resigned, and scrambled again to start a freelance business to support my family.

I'd spent so much time trying not to get hit by closing doors that I lost the ability to see the open doors God was putting in my path.

If you've seen *Monsters, Inc.* you know what I mean when I say the journey I've been on has felt like the climactic scene of that movie. Mike, Sulley, and Boo are dangling from the conveyer belt filled with thousands of doors, and all those doors are just within reach. But they can't open just any door. Walking through the wrong door could put them in a blizzard or in the heat of a desert. Opening the right one would take them home. So they hang on with all their strength, fighting the enemy who sought to distract and destroy, until they can reach the one door they know means safety and security.

The internet gives us the ability to see the doors God is opening for other people around the world, and we lose sight of the one door God wants us to step through in faith. Not every door is meant for us. Not every door leads us home.

As I let go of the crazy conveyer belt of options and stepped back from striving, God showed me an idea that changed everything. I had been looking for the doors that would be good for me, the best use of my skills, the impressive doors that would lead to "bigger and better." Unlike the doors in *Monsters, Inc.*, ones that might lead us to the middle of a snowstorm or a faraway desert, often there are no bad choices. In those seasons of selfish striving, I may have been working for myself, but God was faithful to continue to work in me.

The lessons we learn, the skills we acquire, the people we meet, and the growth we experience can all be blessings. God has given us the free will to choose the doors we go through without worrying that we'll find ourselves outside of God's will on the other side. We may not find ourselves in the perfect profession, or doing work that feels like it aligns with our calling, but God will meet us there. Whichever door I chose, wherever I found myself when it opened, God wanted me to serve instead of striving.

Ortberg says "open-door people are blessed to bless."[2] Ortberg sees God's promise to Abram in Genesis 12:2-3 as "an opportunity to know and experience God, and that included being used by God to enhance others. Abram is called to build his life on this offer: that he can receive a gift from God, but only if he allows his life to become a gift to others."[3] When we believe God's vision for our lives, we need to also believe we are to use those opportunities to lift others.

Holy hustle is about changing our thinking from
"What's in it for me?" to "How can I serve?"

As nice as that all sounds, it can be extraordinarily difficult. And that's why I believe serving others is a superpower God gives us to build, strengthen, and use for His glory.

Superheroes might be able to fly or use super strength to save people, but we have something better. We have Jesus living inside of us, the Savior of the world, ready to work through us to bring His salvation message to our families, neighbors, and communities. When we use the gifts God has given us, the talents He has built into our very beings, and we use them in ways that benefit others instead of just our bank accounts, we put our superpowers into action.

I happen to love a phrase that commonly bounces around social media: "A rising tide lifts all boats." Think of the superpower of service like that. When you decide to see the open door God has placed before you as an opportunity to use your work to serve others, you create a ripple in the water. It might not look like much to you from your perspective on the shore, but that ripple continues and grows and turns into a wave as the very people God has put in your life begin to serve others because you first served them. That wave becomes a rising tide that gently lifts others along the way, putting them in positions to use their talents to serve God or to finally be in the right place to see the next door God wants to open for them. Just like the seeds we often sow in faith, unable to physically experience the harvest God has planned, these little ripples done in our small-moment obedience are often just the first step in God's abundant plan.

Has anyone in your life served you with their gifts in a way that has encouraged you to work hard and rest well for God's glory? As much time as I spend on social media, I've found myself drawn specifically to conferences, ministries, and individuals who use their superpower of service (and position, platform, and programs) to give others the opportunity to shine. Their holy hustle goes beyond getting the items on their "to-do" lists checked off each day, or promoting new content or creating new products. They love well through their work and honor God through their hustle.

I think of day care staff like Heidi, Cortney, and Melanie, who spend their days wrangling toddlers and preschoolers to teach them about the love of Jesus. Friends like Angela, who is acutely aware of both her friends' talents and her organization's needs, and makes space for people to use their gifts to give back and serve children. Women like my pastor's wife, who loves to encourage women to use their gifts in big and small ways, from serving publicly to organizing the church library or using their design skills to create beautiful signs. College ministry workers who spend evenings and weekends showing impressionable young adults how to use their gifts in the world with integrity. Business owners who hire the homeless or commit a portion of their profits to support a nonprofit that gives others the opportunity to one day own a business. Families who sponsor a child in need despite the impact the monthly donation has on their already tight budget. Little kids who use their creativity and courage to run lemonade stands because they want to make a difference too.

The superpower of service gives us the opportunity to make an impact for God's kingdom through faithful, small acts as we serve others every day.

It's typically easy for me to come up with a list of the women I admire who do this well, but as I sat down at my desk to try to come up with a list of ways I could harness *my* superpower of service, it was harder than I anticipated. It started as a list of tasks that were still mostly about me, which might just be the kryptonite of this particular superpower.

We'll only grow in our abilities when we set aside our agendas and make room for God to shine.

Proverbs 31 offers a clear directive of how to serve others with our gifts. "Speak up for those who have no voice, for the justice of all who are dispossessed. Speak up, judge righteously, and defend the cause of the oppressed and needy" (Proverbs 31:8-9). You know what I love most about that section of Scripture? Right before we dive into the "capable wife" part of Proverbs 31, we get a glimpse into some wise words shared with a king—by his mama. I don't know about you, but some motherly wisdom carries significant weight around our household. King Lemuel's mother was reminding him that he not only had power, but a responsibility to use his role and his work to serve others.

We don't need to hold positions of great power or authority to use where we are and what we have to be a voice for those who have none or defend the needy in our neighborhoods and communities. What are some small ways you might be able to help someone rise this week? As you look at the next set of products you need to create, is there a way to include a new voice or perspective? Could you join forces with your neighbors to use your gifts together to create an experience that gives back to your community? Or maybe you can partner with an organization that is doing incredible work but might need your special skill set to take their message to the next level? If you have a blog, could you offer opportunities there for others to share their stories and expertise? If you run an event, could you invite some fresh faces to the table, to teach or encourage your audience?

When we use our work to serve others, we can honor God as we bring Him the glory instead of shining the spotlight on ourselves.

As we look to Scripture to see how we can serve with our work, it would be a mistake to skip over that well-known "capable wife." Although I'm afraid you might just shut the book and run away when you see where we're going with this one. Are you ready?

May we talk about the Proverbs 31 woman? I know. I *know*. This woman seems perfect and can do it all, and I usually feel intimidated by her when I read this section of Scripture. My life is definitely more "she shops the clearance aisle at Target" than her "clothing is fine linen" (Proverbs 31:22). But I really think God has something to say to us in this passage about holy hustle. This is a woman who works hard and provides for her family. Here's a short list of what the Bible says she has, does, or is:

- selects wool and flax and works with willing hands
- rises while it is still night and provides food for her household
- evaluates a field and buys it
- plants a vineyard with her earnings
- has strong arms
- reaches out to the poor and needy
- prepares for inclement weather
- makes her own sheets
- makes and sells linen garments
- delivers belts to merchants
- watches over the activities of her household
- is never idle

Like Ruth, this unnamed woman in Proverbs 31 is blessed for the work she does with strength, dignity, and honor. And she is clearly an accomplished, talented entrepreneur with a savvy mind for business. The original boss-mama if there ever was one! "Give her the reward of her labor, and let her works praise her at the city gates" (Proverbs 31:31).

May I admit something to you? I'm tired just reading that list of what she does, and to learn that she does it all with a pleasant attitude, her children call her blessed, and her husband praises her. It's almost too much. I wonder if a modern version of her story would also tell us that she shares encouraging live Facebook videos each day, runs a small group at her church, and volunteers on the weekends, all while meal-planning for her Whole 30 clean eating and fitness accountability group.

We'll dig deeper into this particular portion of Scripture at the end of this chapter, because it's important to understand context (and to find out why I think resting well is part of her story, even if it's not explicitly mentioned). If we were to model our lives after everything mentioned in these 21 short verses of Scripture, we would certainly get some work done, but we might also find ourselves applying our worth to our work and comparing our accomplishments to the woman down the street.

When we think about working hard and resting well, we can appreciate that the woman in Proverbs 31 isn't striving after any unnecessary work. That's the difference between how the world views hustle and how we can embrace holy hustle. The world would tell her serving her family and her home isn't good enough—she should be doing more, making more money, serving larger audiences, and making a name for herself.

For some of us, in some seasons, God may call us to serve in some of those larger and more public ways when He knows our souls can bear the cost. Holy hustle isn't about striving to do more; it's about settling into the lane God has called us to and working for Him with everything we have. The woman in this Scripture knows which gifts and talents God has given her, and she uses them to serve her family and her community. The door God has opened for her includes using her creativity to make beautiful items that she can enjoy, that her family can use, and that her community will purchase. She is a good steward of her finances, not heading out on a shopping spree but investing in what will become a legacy for her family.

I want it to be a joy to serve my family, to work hard to maintain a safe space for my husband and daughter to come home to each day. I want to do the work God gives me with a happy heart, working to honor Him and provide for my family. And when I start looking for more, neglecting the ministry right in front of me, or becoming idle in serving my loved ones, that's my red flag that I have, again, started striving. Because the key verse in this Scripture isn't found in the list of items this woman does, but in for whom she works.

In the *She Reads Truth Bible*, Rebecca Faires writes this about the Proverbs 31 woman: "Rather than be overawed by this extraordinary list, we can submit ourselves to Christ and begin faithfully with the small things…Every day, average obedience in the same direction is the simple thing that changes the world."[4] The work of the woman in this passage is extraordinary, not because of her hustle, but because it is an outpouring of God's power in her. And we have that same superpower available in us if we're willing to move our pride out of the way and walk through the ordinary-looking door God has placed right in our path.

---

*Holy hustle is only and always about
shining the spotlight on God.*

Digging Deeper

Read Proverbs 31:10-31

Because of sections of Scripture like this one, you might find me at a local seminary one day, learning to read the Old Testament in its original language. I want to know what this sounds like as an alphabet acrostic, to hear the significance of the words that were chosen as they line up in a specific order for the reader. What a beautiful way to end the book of Proverbs, with this poem highlighting a wife who works hard, provides for her family, and is honored, above all, because she loves God.

The strength of the woman in this section stands out. What a wonderful example of serving instead of striving, relying more on the strength of God and His provision than on her own power. It might be easy to miss as we skim through this section or hear it read to us, yet again, at a Mother's Day service at church. Yes, this woman (I wish she had a name. I want to call her Jane. Or maybe Ann.) accomplishes a lot with the time and talents she has at her disposal, but she is praised because she fears the Lord, not because she hustles ceaselessly.

"Strength" seems to be a reoccurring theme in this passage. In verse 15 we read, "she rises while it is still night and provides food for her household," and my *Holman Christian Study Bible* notes that, in this case, "food" means "prey, implying diligence, strength, and cunning."[5] Verse 17 says, "She draws on her strength and reveals that her arms are strong." This was not a woman who sat behind a desk in a fancy home and ordered other people to do the work for her. "It requires tremendous strength to earn the extra money to buy a vineyard, then to clear it of stones, plant the vines, dig a winepress, and build a tower to protect it."[6] The more I read about her, this capable wife, the more I admire her strength, determination, and ability to honor God with her gifts by serving her family. She knew her work mattered. She knew faithfully doing the hard work of planting that vineyard would one day result in a blessing for her children and their children that would continue to provide for their needs. She didn't need to be invited to a fancy conference, speak in front of thousands of people, or have her name in lights to feel worthy of her calling.

She knew her strength was from God,
and she woke up and did the work.

Beyond the specific tasks mentioned in this section, which can make us feel like we're simply piling more "to do" items on our packed agendas, this section of Scripture can serve as a reminder to honor God, serve our families, and work hard right where we are. We don't need to put pressure on ourselves to complete these exact tasks—I promise I'm still going to go buy our clothing and bedding from a store—but we can be encouraged and inspired by her holy hustle.

This Proverbs 31 woman already lived in a lovely home, with servants and enough money to buy imported food. She had a husband who was well known throughout the city. She may not have needed to do these tasks. But she was a woman after God's own heart, and she knew idleness is not in line with God's nature. So she worked hard, but she worked wisely.

Strength may have been the first theme to jump out at me in this reading, but wisdom was a close second. This amazing woman isn't noted for pulling an all-nighter and multitasking uselessly. She looks at the work before her and the potential profit, evaluates the products she can create at a higher quality than what she can buy, and she moves forward with activities that will be a blessing to her family.[7] We are all capable of doing so many things. Our culture tells us we can be anything we want and achieve anything we desire, if we simply work hard enough.

God may have equipped us to be able to do anything,
but He does not expect us to do everything.

A wise woman, a Proverbs 31 woman, looks at the opportunities she has to serve and to work, and with wisdom that comes from abiding closely with the Father, she prioritizes her tasks so she can accomplish the best.

This passage of Scripture might initially make us feel like we're required to do *all the things* to be considered capable or blessed. But what we need to do is serve God with our whole hearts, following His plan for our lives and our work, and rely on Him for the strength and wisdom we need to do it. Our superpower of serving with our gifts doesn't come from our own willpower, but from God's power in us. This is a woman who kept herself so close to God and His plan for her family that she had no time to look around to see what any of the other women in her town were doing. Matthew Henry points out that "she does not intermeddle in the concerns of other people's houses; she thinks it enough for her to look well to her own." She didn't have time for busy work to make herself look impressive, and she didn't have a minute to waste on anything other than working hard right where God had called her. When we can abide with God and work hard for His glory, one day we might also be viewed as having "strength like the young and honor like the old" as our lives show that "the end reward of wisdom depends on its beginning: the fear of the Lord."[8]

Although some scholars think this section of Proverbs 31 was written by a different author and not connected to verses 1 through 9, which we touched on earlier, it's interesting to discover a connection between King Lemuel's mama's instructions to "defend the cause of the oppressed and needy" (verse 9) and the way our capable wife reaches "out to the poor, and she extends her hands to the needy" (verse 20). This idea of "reaching out" encourages me to stop waiting for others to ask for my help or to invite me to use my gifts, but to remain actively aware of the people and opportunities God places before me. We might be most comfortable serving those we know and love, but how much more could we do for God's kingdom by offering those same gifts to our neighbors, community, local church, and the world?

This woman works hard, serves others, and is a delight to be around. She laughs easily and speaks wisely. She doesn't pursue the praise of others but trusts that the work she completes and the words she speaks will result in praise from the only One who matters. Although it doesn't specifically tell us that she rests, I think we can assume a woman who walked with the Lord would honor the Sabbath, resting well when the work was done. When we use our gifts to serve instead of striving, we find peace in the role God has given us. We stay focused on the path God has for us, content with our place and our purpose, trusting God's timing and provision with abundant joy.

Holy Hustle Story

KATE: GRANDMOTHER

I've always been a "get it done" kind of person. I haven't always had a lot of patience for lazy people or ones who have so much to offer but just aren't doing anything productive. I hate to waste time! That said, God will bring people like me into seasons when working, doing, and constantly accomplishing will have to go by the wayside for a while. More than anything, I've tried to take the pressure off myself and focus more on what God wants me to do rather than on what I want to get done. I'm trying to make it about His priorities, not mine. It's not always easy, but obedience is always right.

For me, holy hustle means giving your all to what God says is important. It's doing your work, living your life, loving your family and friends in obedience to Him, not to some random standard the world has set, not in competition with other women. It's hearing His voice for your life and resting in that. I guess I could sum it up like this: living fully without striving. And when I start to forget to work and serve in that space, I turn back to Psalm 23. Truly, this psalm has saved my life. "The LORD is my shepherd, I shall not want. He makes me lie down in green pastures. He leads me beside the still waters. He restores my soul" (Psalm 23:1-3 NKJV). He does the leading, and when we follow, He restores and renews.

Reflection

Are you ready to grab that superhero cape from your closet and start serving? It can be a challenge to reframe our view of something as humble as serving others into something that feels extraordinary, but think about the ways Jesus came to serve. God makes the humble things holy, and when we stop making our work about ourselves and shine the light on God, even our most mundane, ordinary tasks can make an incredible impact for His kingdom.

I hope learning more about our friend in Proverbs 31 has encouraged and inspired you as you consider where God might want you to focus your holy hustle. When we walk closely with God, staying rooted in His Word and giving Him full reign over our agendas, we can work with strength, wisdom, and joy. We can trust Him to open the right doors, at the right time, and we can notice the opportunities right in front of us as we stop looking around to see what everyone else is doing. Consider letting go of your white-knuckle grip on that spinning conveyer belt of opportunity and rest for a moment, asking God to show you your next right step. The Proverbs 31 woman didn't do it all, but she did what was right for her family—evaluating, considering, and completing the tasks set before her.

We don't need to do it all—we just need to do all of what God is giving us in this season.

Thinking back over this chapter:

- How would you rewrite Proverbs 31 in your own words, with your own story?

- Do you find yourself appreciating this section of Scripture in a new way, or does this woman's story still overwhelm you?

- Where have you been distracted by the "concerns of other people's houses" and neglected your own?

- What superpower of service could you put into action today for your family, your neighbors, your workplace, your church, or your community?

- If you've been serving, what have been the biggest struggles and the greatest blessings?

- What open doors have you missed as you've focused on bigger and better instead of right-here obedience?

If you've been quietly discounting yourself from this conversation because your work life doesn't look a certain way, get ready. We're about to jump into a chapter that will challenge your definition of work as we discover how to outdo one another in a way that honors God. As we get ready to do that, lean into the promise of Psalm 23 that Kate shared with us. Trust God to lead you, and as you walk with Him, allow yourself to discover rest and restoration so you can continue to faithfully say yes to the work He has for you.

⬦⬦◊◊◊

_____

_____

_____

_____

_____

_____

_____

_____

_____

_____

Anything You Can Do, I Can Do Better

*Do one thing at a time. Do it well. Or just get it done.
Done is better than perfect, and doing one thing well
is better than doing a thousand mediocre things.*

LARA CASEY

If you and I could sit down and talk about the work we do, I wonder if we would eventually come around to the part of our conversation where we talk about whether the world considers the tasks we do, "work." It has become common to hear discussions on morning television and blogs about the "mommy wars" and how to avoid comparison with mothering styles. "You do you" is thrown around in creative circles to encourage women to focus on their own work without trying to fit into a certain format. "Stay in your own lane" is what we hear in faith circles to keep one another on track, avoiding the hurt that comes with comparison.

I've never cared about mommy guilt, maybe because I have a feeling I'm one step away from messing it all up anyway. I'll happily listen to encouragement and advice from other moms, but I have no issue ignoring what doesn't work with our family. Yet when it comes to work guilt? Man. My work doesn't look like the typical "30 years of committed service and retiring with a gold watch" job of the previous generation, and it certainly doesn't look anything like what I'd planned. I may not doubt my worth and value as a mama, but I find myself questioning my vocation frequently. Am I doing it well enough? Is it enough for my family? How should I explain my work when someone asks?

When someone asks you if you work, what do you say? When I worked for DaySpring, my grandmother was certain I wrote the copy for their greeting cards because that fit into what she knew about the company (they offer faith-based gifts and greeting cards that she can buy at our local LifeWay) and what I did (I was a writer). No matter how many times I tried to explain my job, the intricacies of the internet and the complexity of a job that required me to do "a little bit of everything" never made sense to a woman who still fondly recalls her days as our local township supervisor. She knows hard work, she knows me, and fancy titles do absolutely nothing for her. It's frustratingly refreshing.

Here's what I need you to agree with me on before we jump further into this chapter and explore what it means to "compete" the way God intends: your work matters. Whatever it is God has called you to do, it's important because He has asked you to do it, not because it's easily explained to the world. Grab your notebook or journal, a blank piece of paper, or open a document on your computer and write down everything you do during the day. Do you keep small people alive? Are you a teacher? Are you gifted with the ministry of availability (my favorite way a blog reader described retirement)? Maybe you're a writer or a storyteller or your neighborhood event planner. Are you a CEO, a receptionist, an accountant, a preacher, a fitness instructor, or a mail carrier? Write down all the work you do, and then take a moment to thank God for the role He's given you in His kingdom.

The message of holy hustle is for everyone,
because everyone has work to do that honors God.

On the bottom of that list, write the words "I'm not enough." I know. I don't like to do it either, because I really enjoy the messages in magazines and books that tell me I can do it! I'm enough! I can make my dreams come true! But the truth is we can never be enough, not when we're focusing on the tasks God is giving us to do. We will sin and fail and forget. We will make it about ourselves, and we will slide into striving as we find ourselves subtly manipulating the situation to benefit our goals and agendas.

But Jesus is more than enough to fill in all our weaknesses with His strength. Let's continue in this next part of our conversation with the freedom that God doesn't expect us to achieve perfection apart from Christ. In Matthew 5:48, Jesus directs us to "be perfect, therefore, as your heavenly Father is perfect." He reminds us that even unbelievers are kind and loving toward people they get along with, but God has created us for more. We are to love both our neighbors and our enemies, going above and beyond in our generosity. We are created in God's image to reflect His perfection, and He gave us the Law in the Old Testament to guide us. When we couldn't achieve that perfection, failing in our obedience, our love, our serving, God sent His Son to earth. Jesus, in His perfect obedience to the Law on our behalf, bridged the gap.

One of my favorite devotional books says it like this: "You formed me, molded me, and carefully crafted every detail of my persona for Your glory. Lord, it is through You that I have identity. The value of my life exists because of You. Thank You. Because of this, there is nothing I can do, right or wrong, to change who I am. There is no title, position, or possession that adds or subtracts to whose I am. In You, my worth is found."[1]

◇◇◇◇◇

I remember the first time I heard the phrase "anything you can do, I can do better." I was a little girl to whom those sounded like fighting words, a call to arms to outdo my enemy in whatever they were doing. I wanted to be the best at the things that mattered to me, which meant reading the most books (or at least claiming that I'd read the books others were talking about so I didn't look stupid), getting the best grades, or doing just a little bit better than someone else on a test. When I knew I wasn't going to be the best—usually in anything that happened in gym class—I simply put up a wall of indifference. *Sure, you can be the best at cartwheels. I have more important things to do.*

How did I ever have friends?

Is that elementary-school phrase still living and active in your life? When we look around at our relationships, our social media circles, our workplaces, does it feel like there is still an unspoken "anything you can do, I can do better" challenge? In those seasons when I've become aware of my burnout and striving, it's because I've silently accepted the challenge presented by the world and attempted to keep up. Now the Joneses live on Instagram and the photos always have better filters on the other side of the fence.

If your email inbox is anything like mine, it's filled with daily invitations to courses, classes, and events that will teach you how to use your gifts to make money, grow your platform, and be the best in your niche. But I believe Christians need to be in the world, using our gifts to shine a light into dark corners and not "preaching to the choir," and I believe our work is valuable and should support our families. Our friend in Proverbs 31 certainly made money with the work she did with those strong arms, so we can stop giving away our work for free.

But somewhere in our hustle we need to remain humble, working for God, and letting go of our desire to be the best. A friend shared this with me one day: "I have totally felt the urge to quit *everything* in the face of perceived pressure and/or people doing it so much 'better' (or at least bigger) than I am. It's kind of strange to think that using social media to simply connect and share our lives goes against the grain of what most people do." At the end of the day, we still have that elementary-school desire to be the best at something. We want our kids to be the stars on their sports team or the smartest in class, and we want to be recognized for being the reason our company hit that big goal or having the best curb appeal on the block. Growing God's kingdom will leave a legacy lasting beyond anything we could ever dream of creating.

Scripture has something to say to us about how we can apply the youthful challenge of "anything you can do, I can do better" to our lives as adults. Romans 12:10 instructs us to "outdo one another in showing honor." *The Message* says it like this: "Love from the center of who you are; don't fake it. Run for dear life from evil; hold on for dear life to good. Be good friends who love deeply; practice playing second fiddle."

Practice playing second fiddle. I played the clarinet from fourth grade until my senior year of high school, mostly because it was a smaller instrument and I wanted to be in the band because of the trip to Disney World I knew we would take. I was also a big fan of the gym class assigned to all band students; I was in my element surrounded by fellow musicians, artists, and non-athletes. The trumpet was the fun instrument my sister chose. The flute was too wimpy for me (and frankly, I couldn't play it at all). The tuba was far too large, and the saxophone seemed to be the cool kid in the room I wasn't nearly qualified enough to attempt. The clarinet, then, with all its squeaky notes and terrible-tasting wooden reeds, became my constant companion for ten years.

Somehow in high school I found myself as the first-chair clarinet. I say "somehow" because I never practiced. I was grateful to have a natural ability to read music and picked up on the songs quickly, but after the charm of learning the instrument in those early elementary years wore off, I rarely spent time refining my skills. I recorded my blind audition cassette each year hoping I simply wouldn't be the worst, and I was pleasantly surprised each year to find my position inching from the row of second clarinets, to first clarinets, and then finally, first-chair clarinet.

It meant I was the best of my section. It also meant that one of my responsibilities was to walk on stage during concert season, play a perfectly in-tune middle C, which was the signal to the rest of the band that they were to join me and begin the performance. It was a terrifying responsibility that put me in the spotlight (literally), which made any off-key note or rough squeak even more obvious. My mistakes and failures were as public as my success.

Playing second fiddle means acknowledging that, although we might be the best, we care more about other people and helping them succeed than about our own position. When our lives reflect Christ, we can compete by outdoing one another with honor, love, and respect. Our work, titles, and roles come in second to our ability to serve the people God has put in our path. Since we've already spent some time digging into serving versus striving, grab what you were working on earlier and let's see if we can come up with a few ways we can apply "anything you can do, I can do better" to outdoing one another in a loving, Christ-honoring way.

What would it look like to extravagantly honor those you work with? What changes to your attitude would need to take place for you to outdo your coworkers, family, or neighbors with respect? Beside the jobs you've listed, make a few notes about where you've found yourself striving to be the best, and about how you can choose love and grace in those circumstances. What words might you want to say to someone this week to show them you see, know, and honor them simply for being the person God created them to be? Maybe it means forgiving a past hurt, even if they haven't apologized. Or maybe it means acknowledging that you aren't the best person for that promotion, or recommending a friend for a speaking opportunity you were tempted to take for yourself despite an unsettled feeling in your heart about saying yes. Competition in the kingdom of God means using the gifts, talents, and tools He's given us to make His name great while honoring those around us—playing second fiddle "better" than anyone else.

It's hard to find a business that still stands by the adage "the customer is always right." My battles with customer service representatives lately read more like "the customer is rarely right and it's our job to make sure we don't give them an inch." Except for Chick-fil-A. You've experienced it, haven't you? You jump in the drive-thru lane to order some chicken minis (those biscuits are everything) and find yourself smiling. You were prepared to wait, to repeat yourself, to have a fuzzy speaker conversation with a high school student who wanted to make sure you knew they didn't want to be there and they *definitely* didn't want to answer your question about whether you could substitute a frozen coffee for an orange juice.

Instead you order, say "Thank you," and hear "It's our pleasure."

You are thanked as you pay, and the cashier at the window makes eye contact and engages with your family. You feel like a person and not just an order number, and you're handed your food with a smile and a directive to have a great day.

Kindness matters. It makes a difference, and in our work it helps us stand apart from the crowd. When we're willing to slow down and treat people like they're more than a sale or stepping-stone to our personal growth goals, we're doing business in a way that honors God because we're honoring relationships. God cares about people and tells us to love our enemies (Matthew 5:44), love our neighbors (Matthew 22:39), and love one another (John 13:34). Loving others well not only creates beautiful, lasting relationships that will also benefit our work, but draws others closer to the kind of life-changing love they can receive only from Jesus.

That trip through a Chick-fil-A drive-thru might start as a breakfast run for biscuits, but when your curiosity gets the better of you and you research why their culture is so different from other fast-food chains, you won't scroll far on the About page of their website before you're reading about the founder's desire to give employees a chance to worship on Sundays with their families. Scroll a bit further and you'll learn their corporate purpose is "To glorify God by being a faithful steward of all that is entrusted to us and to have a positive influence on all who come into contact with Chick-fil-A." They treat people differently to honor a God who sees the value in all people.

◇◇◇◇◇

We sat on the folding chairs of our church gym one Sunday morning, having chosen to attend the more contemporary service instead of our usual service in the sanctuary. With five Sunday morning services to choose from, our church has found a way to be good stewards of their space, resources, and community by offering options that are inviting to everyone while maintaining the same strong Scripture-based messaging throughout their ministries. You might be in a gym with a preacher wearing jeans, but you will hear the gospel preached as clearly as in the sanctuary with a pastor wearing dress pants and a tie.

Last Sunday my husband and I were listening to a powerful message about generosity. At the end of the service we were asked to share what we would do if we found $100—ours to spend any way we liked. What did our family need most at that very moment? How would $100 change our circumstances? Listeners shared a few ideas—home improvement projects, new clothes for school, a meal to share with extended family. Across the room a woman spoke through tears. She would use the money to take her children away for a night to a hotel with a pool so they could laugh and play and be away, just for a few hours, from the abuse and fear of the night before. It was stunningly honest, vulnerable, and heartbreaking.

The pastor called her to the front, pulled $100 out of his wallet, and gave it to her. No strings attached. "You have no idea. You have no idea," she sobbed. Church members in the seats nearby rose and surrounded her, a wall of prayer and support building around her as she wept. It was unplanned and unexpected, but a powerful challenge.

Would you do it? Would you use $100 for no other purpose than to outdo someone in honor and love by blessing them when God says "Give"? Whether you happen to have the money already in your wallet, or you need to save for six months, can we decide together to take the challenge? As we do the work God has given us, let's be good stewards of the resources He provides and show others that holy hustle is different because we care more about people than platforms.

Kindness matters.

Digging Deeper

Read Romans 12

Like all of Paul's writings, the book of Romans was written in response to the "problems and needs of local churches." But because Paul hadn't yet been to Rome when he wrote this letter, my Bible's study notes go on to say, it's believed he may have had a larger audience in mind.[2] Paul's words about unity, truth, and salvation may have been intended for the early church, but they are also incredibly applicable for us today.

When we read all of Romans 12, not just the small piece of it we touched on earlier, we find living in a way that allows us to outdo one another with honor begins with personal transformation. Before we ever get to a Scripture about how to live with or love another person, Paul instructs, "Do not be conformed to this age, but be transformed by the renewing of your mind, so that you may discern what is the good, pleasing, and perfect will of God" (Romans 12:2).

Putting others first is countercultural to the age we live in. As I scrolled through Instagram the other day, I saw a post that said, "That's the problem with putting others first. You've taught them that you come second."[3]

In holy hustle, putting others first isn't a problem; it's the whole point.

In those seasons when I've chosen to put myself first and conform to culture's view of success, I have found myself striving, fighting, and defending to make sure no one would ever think I could be anything but the best. I was afraid of helping someone too much because I thought that meant I would be needed less. Before we get to the point where we can outdo others with honor, we need to start here—renewing our minds, transforming our thoughts, and leaning further into a version of success that doesn't just mean personal victories, but kingdom growth.

In case we needed the "humble" part of living a holy hustle lifestyle confirmed, in the next verse Paul makes sure we know we should not think more highly of ourselves than we should, but to understand that the gifts, talents, and work God has given each of us work together to serve His kingdom (Romans 12:3-5). "Paul exhorts Christians to be humble and to use what God has given for the good of the body" and then lists some practical ways the early church could use their gifts to assist those in need in their communities, doing so with generosity, diligence, and cheerfulness.[4]

When we transform our minds away from the "me first" perspective of the world and embrace a "God first, others second" view of our work, we can stop competing and comparing and instead choose contentment. The work we do, the way we use our gifts, and the ways we honor others can come from a place of joy instead of a place of jealousy when we swap striving for serving. We'll dig deeper into the ways collaboration and community play a key role in holy hustle in the next chapter.

Only now, when our minds are focused on God's will and our hands are involved in doing the work we have been gifted to do, can we start looking outward and learning how to engage with our neighbors. Paul is a writer after my own heart, getting straight to the point without all the fluff. His directives in verses 9 through 18, taken from the *Holman Christian Standard Bible*, read like a bulleted journal list:

- Love must be without hypocrisy.
- Detest evil.
- Cling to what is good.
- Show family affection to one another.
- Outdo one another in showing honor.
- Do not lack diligence.
- Be fervent in spirit.
- Serve the Lord.

- Rejoice in hope.
- Be patient in affliction.
- Be persistent in prayer.
- Pursue hospitality.
- Bless those who persecute you.
- Rejoice with those who rejoice.
- Weep with those who weep.
- Be in agreement with one another.
- Do not be proud.
- If possible, on your part, live at peace with everyone.

Living this way, loving others and serving God? It takes a tremendous amount of work. It's far easier to choose the version of this list that lines up with what the rest of the world is doing. It's less work to be apathetic, to ignore the needs of others, to do work that honors ourselves, and to judge others. Yet we are not called to the easy life, but to the holy life. On our own, in our own strength, Paul's list feels impossible. And it is. We will fail when we try to do it all on our own. But when we take time each day to refocus our minds on the good, pleasing, and perfect will of God, we can do the hard work of humbling ourselves and putting others first. Jill McDaniel writes, "Spiritual disciplines are rooted in the Spirit's work in us. God is the Giver. We are the recipients. He empowers. We surrender."[5]

<><><><>

I have known for a long time now that I was born with a strong desire for justice. When things don't appear to be fair, I fight back. I spent time working with a social justice organization at Villanova, raising money to build wells for those who need clean water in Waslala, Nicaragua, joining all the 5ks. (To walk, not run. Let's not be crazy.) When I first heard about St. Jude Children's Research Hospital, I immediately signed up to raise money for their yearly all-night event on college campuses—and I did so for several years with friends. And when someone steals my idea, copies my work, or creates a similar product after we've talked about my dreams? It takes everything I have not to jump online and tell the world how unfair it is, retaliating for the hurt and betrayal my heart feels.

Paul addresses this too. And for those of us who work in a creative field and struggle with the reality that there is truly nothing new under the sun, this is an important reminder. "The normal response is to retaliate, but Christians are called to serve and minister God's grace to a lost and hostile world. Jesus is our model. As much as possible, we are to live at peace with everyone...God is the judge and administrator of wrath. Our role is to display God's grace and love in our lives. God in Jesus conquered evil on the cross. We are not to let evil conquer us."[6]

We are called to be weird, to live differently and respond in a way that makes others look at us and see Jesus. That doesn't mean we shouldn't know how to protect our ideas and our work, because we are also called to be good stewards of what God has given us—including our talents. But we can work confidently, with grace and peace and honoring others, because we know God will take care of the judgments. We just need to work hard, rest well, do good, and love others.

Holy Hustle Story

ERIN: FIVE-TIME CANCER SURVIVOR

I've always loved the word *hustle*, mostly because as an athlete I absolutely hated to run. Long distance, I mean. I was all about short, quick bursts of energy paired with focus on honing specific skills by practicing them—correctly first, and then on repeat until they clicked. When God called us to start our ministry, my husband and I were both working full-time jobs in other industries. At the beginning, our hustle was more about making little bits of slow progress in between the traditional work we were already doing. Being constrained by time, energy, and a steep learning curve was a blessing in those early days because we had to rely on guidance we received in prayer and time spent together talking about what God was doing and how we were going to be a part of it.

We both learned a lot during that early time of slow hustle because we had spent so much time in the corporate world trying to be as fast and efficient as possible. Honestly, we've learned that God can do more with us hustling slow than He can with us grinding and pushing through, focused on our own strength.

When it comes to the idea of "holy hustle," I would define it as the diligent pursuit of God-breathed goals with the ultimate goal being growing in relationship with Him. Psalm 62:1 is the verse I turn to when I need to stay focused on the work God has given us, and the slow hustle that comes from resting in His timing: "I am at rest in God alone; my salvation comes from Him."

Reflection

Are we okay getting a little weird for Jesus in our hustle? I remember years of trying so desperately to balance the desires to fit in and stand out in school. I never wanted to be seen as different, but I also wanted to be unique and special. Well, here's our chance to show our teen selves that different is good and unique is part of who God created us to be. God's creation has no cookie-cutter people. Our fingerprints tell the truth about a creator God who is so infinitely creative that even that small piece of our identity is special, different from every other person's on the planet. But not only our fingerprints identify who we are. Our reactions, the way we treat others, and our attitudes as we work are distinguishing features that tell the world more than who we are. They tell *whose* we are.

When it comes to competition, how does it make you feel to know that God asks us to outdo one another? Is it uncomfortable to think about putting others first? List the emotions and gut-level reactions you're having. Are you afraid you'll be overlooked if you put others first? Is this an exciting challenge you can't wait to tackle?

Maybe you're uncomfortable with the thought of outdoing someone, even in honor, because you're a people-pleaser (recovering or otherwise). Or maybe you find yourself feeling a little bit bitter about this directive, because you feel like you've always been the kind of person who puts others first, only to be walked all over, taken advantage of, left behind. Or you're wondering when someone is going to put *you* first.

I find myself alternating between all those reactions as well as a few others when I think about this piece of holy hustle. But as I lean into the hustle the way God defines it, and I start to adopt a lifestyle that serves instead of strives, it all starts to come together. We call our skills and abilities "gifts" for a reason. They were generously and graciously chosen specifically for us by God, the One who knows us better than anyone else. He knows what we can do with them if we give Him the chance to direct our steps.

This week take a step back from your hustle and ask God to renew and transform your mind. Before you get to work each day, ask God to open your eyes to His agenda for the day. As difficult situations with others come up, ask Him to give you words filled with grace and love, and then hand the judgments and fights over to Him, believing that He will take care of it all. Ask God to show you who He wants you to honor this week, and practice playing second fiddle as you work, rest, and love others with grace and love.

◇◇◇◇◇

_____

_____

_____

_____

_____

_____

_____

_____

_____

_____

_____

_____

_____

_____

_____

_____

_____

_____

Choosing Community

*Friendship is an opportunity to act on God's
behalf in the lives of the people that we're close
to, reminding each other who God is.*

SHAUNA NIEQUIST

t takes a village—not only to raise a child, but to turn our ordinary hustle into something holy and glorifying to God.

Comparison. Competition. Community. When I look at the bossy messages of hustle the world screams at us, comparison means proving to our audience why they should choose us instead of our competitors. Competition means striving ceaselessly to ensure our product, work, or words are not only the best, but the most unique and available before anyone else's. It screams "I was here first!" And community? Well, that's just a nice word for customers who become the targets of our advertising, marketing, and email newsletters.

After working in marketing for more than ten years, I get it. My brain tends to fall back into those same definitions when I forget the purpose behind my work. Instead of serving, I start selling, and in the process I value profits over people. But there is a different way. In a holy hustle economy, comparison means looking at our own work and asking God to show us how it does—or does not—line up with His will. How do our lives compare to the life of Christ we're meant to model? Competition isn't about making sure we win, but, as we addressed in the last chapter, looking for ways to help others rise, outdoing them in honor. And community is the essential ingredient that sets holy hustle apart from the way the rest of the world works. It looks more like collaboration, care, and conversation than targeting customers.

Now that we've redefined hustle (to work rapidly or energetically for God's kingdom), we've explored God's model of work, and we've read some compelling examples from Scripture regarding hustle, what do we do? What if our fears and insecurities paralyze us and keep us from doing the work God has called us to do? How can working within the community God has given us, to serve without jealousy and comparison, make a difference?

> When two of you get together on anything at all on
> earth and make a prayer of it, my Father in heaven goes
> into action. And when two or three of you are together
> because of me, you can be sure that I'll be there (Matthew
> 18:20 MSG).

Two or three.

It doesn't seem like enough, does it? When we feel bombarded by courses and measures that track success by titles, or a specific number of followers, fans, and subscribers, only two or three seems like a failure.

Have you ever noticed that God doesn't call us to be in just one kind of community? In some seasons I've been part of something big, where the community was several thousand women meeting worldwide for the same reason and connecting because they share a passion for Jesus. I love that so much—the body of Christ, coming together, sisters all worshiping together. And I've been called to attend conferences, joining several hundred women who all share a passion for using their God-given gifts to change the world while having fun on Twitter and eating chocolate and cupcakes.

But when it comes down to it? When we look at the kind of community that draws us deeply, consistently, authentically, reliably to God? The small moments count. Those two people God puts in our path in the most ordinary of places sometimes become the biggest blessing.

It's the one-on-one friendship with a mentor who loves me enough to tell me truth that isn't comfortable, the one who holds me accountable in the comfort of her home and loves my child as much as I do. It's the friends who have decades of history with me, always there on the other side of my social media messages, ready with an encouraging word, cheer, prayer, or note to tell me, "No, you can't give up."

It's no easier to invite others to join you on your journey than it is to practice playing second fiddle. When our hearts have experienced the hurt of broken friendships, or we've watched someone receive credit for our work, or we've felt betrayed by those we trusted, it can feel far easier to go on the defensive and work alone.

I recently struggled with lower back pain. After several relaxing but unproductive trips to the chiropractor, it wasn't until I was sharing with my counselor that I realized what I'd been doing. Immediately following my unplanned resignation from ministry work, I went into survival mode. Instead of asking for help, I pushed forward. Instead of trusting God with my reputation, I unintentionally began bracing myself for whatever I might see that day on the internet—a post about a project I used to work on, an announcement about the launch of a product that was my idea. I was in battle mode, ready to defend myself against anyone's opinion about me, my work, or what they might be saying about me behind my back.

Constantly waiting for the next failure, the next hurt, the next betrayal left me in pain physically, an outward result of an inward struggle. The only way to stop acting out of a place of defensiveness was to start trusting God with my story again and ask others to help me. And starting small was exactly where I needed to be.

What happens when the desire of our hearts to be part of something big meets the call on our lives to dig deeper into the small spaces? Jesus's life teaches us a lot about community. Sure, He had thousands of followers. He changed lives in big ways in big crowds. But the moments that stand out to me are when Jesus was with His closest circle—the Twelve. Or the three. Teaching, praying with, praying for—living life together. When we find ourselves getting caught up in how many people follow us, we lose sight of the fact that we're meant to follow only Jesus. There is a huge blessing in the small.

When two or three are gathered with hearts dedicated to the holy hustle of making God's kingdom great, that's all it takes.

Bob Goff wrote, "We won't be distracted by comparison if we're captivated by purpose."[1] I love community, but I struggle with jealousy and comparison. As God and I have been working through the roots of those issues, untangling lies I've too long believed and truth I didn't think applied to me, I'm learning community can be wonderfully, beautifully messy. As an introvert, I struggle to find a balance between my love for working behind the scenes, by myself, without too much attention, and that strong desire for fairness, to be given credit for work done well. I want to share what I'm working on, but I don't want to brag. I want to tell you about an opportunity God has given me, but I don't want you to feel envious. I want my birthday to be celebrated and for my people to make me feel special, but do not, for the love, bring out a team of people at a restaurant to sing to me.

It might be messy, but community is always worth the hard work. God didn't create us to live life alone, and that applies to our work too. We can do so much more for God's kingdom when we stop competing and start collaborating. I've often turned to this prayer in *Thirty-One Days of Prayer for the Dreamer and Doer* when I needed encouragement to stay in community when it got hard: "I'm so grateful for the opportunities I have to serve You while using the gifts You've given me—especially when it involves working alongside others. It's so encouraging to see a group of people with different, unique abilities coming together and collaborating on a project. It's in moments of opportunities and collaboration that I can't help but praise You for granting me the desires of my heart and partnering me with like-minded believers!"[2]

Whether you meet officially with like-minded creatives in an online mastermind group, attend networking events at your local chamber of commerce, take a weekend to soak in wisdom and teaching at a conference, or have coffee with other moms, investing in community gives us the opportunity to share our God-given gifts with others and to connect with someone who might be able to use their strengths to help our weaknesses.

In my brief time working as a virtual assistant, I discovered my favorite people to work with were other bloggers, writers, and speakers. My goal? To take care of the mundane day-to-day tasks so they could focus on their passion. I loved being able to use my administrative skills, my knowledge of their field, and my ability to quickly create graphics to share their message, course, or product. It was an honor to help carry their burden by doing some of the work alongside them. When we try to do everything ourselves, in whatever role God has given us, we not only begin to believe we are irreplaceable, but we fail to allow others to experience those opportunities to use their gifts to serve, grow, and encourage.

◇◇◇◇◇

Anna lost the race for her team that was competing against another group of teens at camp. She was the final member of her team to take on a massive obstacle course that was, to make things even more challenging, floating in the middle of the pool. Diving, swimming, and climbing over obstacles led the contestants to the final piece of the course—a floating balance beam. Anna was exhausted. She struggled to lift herself up onto the platform. Suddenly, one of her teammates dove in to help hold the raft steady so she could climb on, even though it meant they would both need to complete the balance beam challenge before their team could move on to the last leg of the race.

Anna stepped onto the beam and fell. She tried again, and fell. She was still standing on that platform with her teammate when the other group of teens finished the race and won. When their activities director asked her if she wanted to finish the challenge, even though time was up, her entire team swam out to help her, to cheer for her, to encourage her. She stepped out, knowing they had already lost the race, but unwilling to allow this obstacle to define her. One step at a time, with her team holding the raft steady, she walked across and finished the course to the cheers of every single camper.

This is what can happen when community gathers around to support one another. Holy hustle means allowing your community to help, and that sometimes hustle looks less like full-speed success and more like slow persistence in the face of failure.

Although we might be the last ones to cross the finish line,
our hustle is no less holy than the one who crossed first.

Balance requires keeping our eyes on one steady, unmoving spot. It requires focus, a mind at rest, and a body at work. When we look around to see what everyone else is doing or rush to finish our work so we can jump ahead to the next goal, we might find ourselves stumbling and off-balance. Only by keeping our eyes fixed on Jesus and our minds content with the right-here work we've been called to can we most effectively complete our own race and help others along the way.

During one season of work I found myself struggling deeply with envy, unable to celebrate the achievements, opportunities, and accolades a coworker was experiencing. I felt unseen, overlooked, and ignored. I'd been so focused on wanting what someone else had that I was ignoring the very place God was asking me to use my gifts. Do you remember the analogy I shared at the beginning of our time together—the one about everyone on the stage yelling over the others, yet speaking to no one? That was God's reminder to me that there is a very good reason He has created each of us to do work differently. If every one of us took a spot on those stages and huge platforms, we wouldn't share a message— we would just make useless noise. In my struggle with envy and my own self-centered dreams for myself, the only kingdom that would have grown or received any glory would have been the one I built for myself. When we choose, instead, to work with grateful hearts in the places and spaces we've been called to, we can become beacons of hope, lights that shine brightly instead of useless noise that stands under a spotlight.

As I've gone on this holy hustle journey, sometimes I've found myself paralyzed in fear, unable to act as I attempted to do this "hustle" thing differently. I knew what I wanted to do, I had a never-ending list of projects I could work on, and I knew how I wanted to do them, but I couldn't seem to get started. I was afraid. What if I slid back into striving? What if I forgot to make time to rest? What if I tried it a new way and failed? The enemy of our souls loves when we start to go down that "what if?" road. He can trap us there, paralyzed by choices, fears, and reminders of past failures.

One day I finally sat down and listed all the things holding me back. Putting them in words took them out of my head and freed me to lean into truth. No matter how many doubts or fears I could come up with, I could stand firm in the truth that God would still be God, I would still be His daughter, and He would still have a purpose for me.

Lara Casey wrote, "You know all those things you've always wanted to do? You should go do them."[3] When you look at your vision board, to-do list, or dreams you would like to realize one day, are you going after them with your whole heart, trusting God's timing and purpose? Or are you using a small following, an unimpressive job title, or comparing yourself to others as an excuse to avoid the work set before you? How can you work hard this week toward one of those goals, resting in the knowledge that God will keep His promises in your life? I was so encouraged by this list Lara Casey shared in her book *Make It Happen*:

> Life is too short to wait to do the good things God
>   has put on your heart.
> The things that God purposed for you long before
>   you took your first breath.
> The things that tug at your heart day and night,
>   beckoning you to use your gifts.
> The things that reflect His light.
>   If you see even a glimmer of one of those things, do it…
> Hush the chatter in your head telling you that you
>   aren't enough. In God alone, you are.[4]

◇◇◇◇◇

My husband is a third-grade teacher at a local elementary school, which means each May I start a list of home-improvement projects for him to tackle when summer break finally arrives. A few years ago we decided to fence in our backyard, creating a safe space for our daughter to play with clear boundaries and privacy. The work started long before summer arrived. Inside our garage for several months was a large section of fence along the wall, looming over my car when I climbed out. It was a trial run of that much larger project we would tackle when the ground thawed.

I'd looked at countless images of fences in different sizes, shapes, designs, and patterns. I'd seen photos of the English-style garden my husband wanted to create once the space was defined. Words like *shadow-box* and *lattice* had been incorporated into my vocabulary as we debated the pros and cons of a six-foot fence versus an eight-foot fence. And I spent entirely too much time in the local home improvement store staring blankly at fence posts.

That piece of fence? It wasn't beautiful in our garage. It was in the way, smelled like a lumberyard, left a layer of dust on everything, and took up entirely too much space. I was worried I might pop a tire on a forgotten screw.

I feel like that piece sometimes. A little lost. Sometimes set aside. Unable to connect my work with the larger finished product God can see clearly. In a noisy world where fancier, shinier, and bigger get the glory, I sit in my small town and live my every day wondering if I'm noticed. Or worse, if I'm just in the way.

As I've spent some time wrestling over my motivations for recognition (one of those roots of envy God has been carefully digging out), God has been teaching me to look at my place and position as a gift from Him. He sees the big picture, the whole project, where every screw and board and refining cut will come together in my life to work together for His kingdom.

And sometimes the smallest pieces add the most strength.

If we planned to build that fence using only the largest pieces of lumber and the heaviest posts, it would collapse immediately. Every piece—from the messiest cement to the smallest screw—must work together to create a structure secure and beautiful.

In a holy hustle community, every gift is needed. Our collaboration with one another gives us the opportunity to turn our small obedience into something beautiful that shows the world what it means to work together, to serve side by side with encouragement instead of envy.

But on those days when it feels incredibly easy to be overlooked? When our view of the world from our computers, our offices, our kid's soccer practices, or our board meetings makes us wonder if we're being used in God's plan at all? God has this to say: "I will not forget you. Behold, I have engraved you on the palm of my hands; your walls are continually before me" (Isaiah 49:16 ESV). No matter what, God does not forget you.

- You are not overlooked.
- You are not insignificant.
- You are not less than.
- God sees you. He knows you. He carries your name on His hands.
- You are His.
- You are chosen.
- You are forgiven.
- You are called.
- You are loved.
- You are included.
- You are wanted.

Following the loud, clanging demands and expectations of the world will only make us feel insecure as we compare our place in God's plan to those around us. Let's instead choose to trust God as the Master Craftsman who knows when, how, and why, and which pieces to use to make something beautiful and secure that will last a lifetime.

Become captivated by God's purpose in your life and lean into the work hard, rest well, and live the life of holy hustle God has called you to, right where you are.

Read 1 Corinthians 12

I've sometimes joked to a friend that I often feel like the armpit in the body of Christ. On those days when nothing seems to be going quite right, or I feel like my gifts are too small, or my fears yell louder than God's quiet guiding voice, it's easy to joke away my contributions. When we read a section of Scripture like 1 Corinthians 12, especially verses 14 through 26, we're reminded that God creatively designed us to live and work in community. We need one another, we need to be for one another, and we need to be willing to play the parts God has assigned us so we can be a healthy, fully functioning body of Christ.

Paul wrote his letter to the Corinthian church to offer "specific solutions to specific problems [and] the underlying answer to all of these problems is for the church and its members to live Christ-centered lives."[5] When we begin to compete with one another for the most important roles, positions, or titles, we forget God runs the show. Our responsibility should be on "other duties as assigned," using the gifts and talents we've been given in collaboration with one another to serve others and honor God.

In verses 7 through 10, Paul reminds the Corinthian church that God assigns different gifts to different people, to "produce what is beneficial" (12:7). The Holy Spirit is living and active in all believers, but we are not all assigned the same gifts, talents, or tasks. Although they were being taught by someone who walked with Jesus, the early Christians in Corinth struggled with comparison and competition, just like us. As they started to see the different kinds of gifts God had given to their neighbors, they began to rank them by how public, impressive, or showy each gift appeared.

A talent like speaking in tongues (the ability to speak in another language you didn't previously know to share the gospel) or healing would certainly draw a crowd, while the gift of faith would be a more subtle, personal experience.[6] Our version of a "showy" gift might be getting a promotion, performing in an arena, writing a book, or gaining a huge social media following, yet we still find ourselves ranking our gifts against the gifts of others.

Paul's example of how all the parts of the human body work together is as relevant today as it was in AD 56. You may have read 1 Corinthians 12 in a different translation, but I like reading familiar Scripture in *The Message* paraphrase when I find myself assuming I already know what God wants to say to me as I read.

> If the foot should say, "Because I am not a hand, I do not belong to the body," that would not make it any less a part of the body. And if the ear should say, "Because I am not an eye, I do not belong to the body," that would not make it any less a part of the body. If the whole body were an eye, where would be the sense of hearing? If the whole body were an ear, where would be the sense of smell? But as it is, God arranged the members in the body, each one of them, as he chose (1 Corinthians 12:15-18).

Every part of the body—our physical bodies and our placement in the body of Christ—is exactly where God wanted it. Your role, whatever it is and wherever it is, matters because God assigned you to that place. Regardless of whether we find ourselves in the most "important" or what feels like the least significant place, it's essential that as followers of Christ we remember the value everyone brings to the table so we can outdo one another with honor, collaborate, and live in the kind of community that glorifies God. Our gifts, used without love, are pointless.[7]

The *Theology of Work Bible Commentary* shares this:

> God's kingdom encompasses the whole world, not just the institutions of the church. Believers can and should exercise their giftings in every setting, including the workplace. Many of the giftings named here—such as leadership, service, and discernment—will be of immediate benefit in the workplace. Others will no doubt be given to us as needed to serve God's purposes in whatever work we do. We should by all means develop the giftings we have

been given and use them for the common good in every sphere of life.

In fact, the most important question is not who, where, what, or how we exercise the giftings of God's Spirit. The most important question is why we employ the gifts. And the answer is, "For love." Gifts, talents, and abilities—coming as they do from God—are sources of excellence in our work...If Christians would exhibit these kinds of love in our places of work, how much more productive and enriching would work be for everyone? How much glory would it bring our Lord? How much closer would we come to God's fulfillment of our prayer, "Thy kingdom come on earth"?[8]

Our holy hustle can accomplish only so much when done on our own. But when we choose to outdo one another in honor and love well as we collaborate instead of compete, we can begin to see a small glimpse of purpose God has for our work. Keeping our eyes focused on the One who did not make a mistake when He assigned us our talents will keep our hearts steady and our feet firmly planted as we continue to follow His plan.

Holy Hustle Story

ANDREA: ARTIST

I feel like God redeemed "hustle" when I stopped looking at work as "Ugh, *work*!" but instead as something He has entrusted to me to do. In other words, just because it's "work" doesn't mean I have to view it as a drudgery—I can change my perspective to see my work as a privilege I've been entrusted with. An honor. A high and holy calling. At different times in my life, work has looked different. I've done everything from retail sales, to housecleaning, to event planning, to nonprofit work, and now I'm working full-time as a lettering artist and small business owner. Work is honorable, whatever the title/position, so do it well, for His glory.

When we are mindful of what a holy and wondrous privilege it is to do what He's entrusted us to do, it will change the way we work, lead, love, give, serve, think. *Whatever* we've been entrusted by God to do, I hope we will see it as an honorable and noble thing. We bring Him glory when we are doing what we are called and created to do.

For me, holy hustle is as simple as enjoying the work God has entrusted to me to do. It's still work, it still requires effort, time, persistence, grit, and discipline (and honestly, sometimes it isn't all "fun"). But looking at my work as a privilege that I'm even able to do what He has called me to do can bring a renewed appreciation for work (and the blessing of rest!). Colossians 3:23 in the *Amplified* translation is the Scripture that helps me maintain that work/rest balance:

> Whatever you do [whatever your task may be], work from the soul [that is, put in your very best effort], as [something done] for the Lord and not for men." Whatever it is we're doing—rest, work, play, serving, living—whatever it is, we'll do best when we do it as unto the Lord.

Reflection

Spend some time considering the ways you contribute to the body of Christ. Have you ever doubted your calling, significance, or purpose because you felt like you were too small, messy, or overlooked? What are some practical steps you can take today to remind yourself that you aren't enough, but God is, and so is your small obedience to His plan?

Ask God to show you where you've been competing and comparing. Ask Him to forgive you for your thoughts of envy or jealousy, and make a plan to become fully aware of the opportunities to collaborate with your community over the coming weeks.

◇◇◇◇◇

_____

_____

_____

_____

_____

_____

_____

_____

_____

_____

_____

_____

_____

_____

_____

_____

This Little Light of Mine

Hide not your talents, they for use were made. What's a sundial in the shade?

BENJAMIN FRANKLIN

Something is wrong with the electricity in our home. I don't pretend to understand how any of it works (I can barely figure out how to make the outsides of the walls look beautiful, so I definitely can't tell you about anything on the inside), but I do know the lightbulbs in our home should probably last more than a month. The other day I stood on a chair in my office to replace yet another burned-out lightbulb that had lost its glow far too soon, and as I flipped the switch to test it, I realized how much I need that light.

I'd spent a few days without the overhead light, relying on sunshine from the windows and the dim beam cast from a wall-mounted light across the room. I'd gotten used to working in semidarkness. It wasn't until I took the time to make my light work again, making it shine in the corners and the shadows of the room, that I realized how dark it had become in that space.

In one corner of my office is a poster that says, "Use this space for Your glory, not mine." As that fresh light brightened up my room, it drew my eyes back to that poster, and the prayer of my heart for this space. God has given me the opportunity to work, to serve my family, and this poster is my reminder that what comes from me is a gift from God, and the spotlight, or the glory, belongs to Him.

My own path to holy hustle has felt like a journey through a dimly lit room, wondering where I'm supposed to go next, or why God has me on this particular path. After I was fired from my marketing job at the bank, I was terrified. All I could think about was how I'd failed, how no one would ever want to hire me again, and how I'd ruined seven years of hard work. But it was seven years of shining the light on myself, outdoing others in negative ways that hurt relationships, and missing how God wanted to use me for His glory in that space. I was in it for me. I wanted to be the bright and shining star—and I was, for a season. But it wasn't a role I was meant to maintain. My soul couldn't bear the burden, and I hadn't counted the cost or considered the expectations. We are not meant to be the light, but to be light bearers.

Do you ever wonder if you're doing the right thing? Or if you're really where God wants you? Or if something more or different or better or bigger is somewhere out there for you? Or maybe you wonder if the cost of your calling is worth the moments you feel like you're missing.

So many moments in life feel like we're in a room where all the lights have burned out and we're stumbling around to find a light switch, a candle, or a flashlight to guide our steps. In those moments, trust God. Grab tightly to His outstretched hand and believe He will guide you safely to the next door He has ready for you to step through. The darkness doesn't have to be scary when we can walk with the Light of the World.

But those questions you're asking yourself are legitimate. Your fears and worries shouldn't cause you shame. If we could all sit down together to talk about our work, our passions, and our faith, I would be surprised if anyone said their life has turned out exactly the way they planned. What would you say to a friend at the table who had those questions? Would you tell her she's right, and that she should probably just give up?

I hope not.

We would love her and pray with her. We would encourage her and find ways to tell her that what she's doing is good, and worthy, and valuable, and that if she knows in her spirit that this is where God wants her in this season, then it's no mistake.

I would tell you how firmly I believe God is in the practice of taking the humble and making it holy, and that obedience (not size, fame, or recognition) is what matters in the impact we make through our kingdom work.

God is faithful in all that He does (Psalm 33:4). Where you are, what you're doing, and the people right in front of you whom God has asked you to serve are no mistake. The challenges, disappointments, and failures are no mistake.

God will use every piece of our story to illuminate His glory.

It can be easy to share that encouragement with a friend, but can you whisper that same thought to your own heart and believe it?

I'll be honest. Some days I question what God has me doing—days when everything I do feels like a battle, where I'm pouring out far more than I'm receiving, and I'm running on empty. When words like *weary* and *exhausted* are part of my vocabulary, it's a sign that some part of the "work hard, rest well" lifestyle of holy hustle is off-balance and I've started to blaze my own trail off the well-marked path God has planned for me.

My husband is an Eagle Scout who grew up going on bike rides and ten-mile hikes through the local woods, Gettysburg parks, and parts of the Appalachian Trail. After a recent picnic lunch with his parents in a local state park, we decided to go for a hike on an easy trail, just to explore the area. Almost immediately, Madi noticed the painted squares on the trees. Matt explained the area had several hiking trails, and that the different colored squares painted on the trees told us which trail we were on. Madi declared herself the official trail marker guide and made it her job to search for and call out every tree marked with the correct paint color. She knew the path would be safe, and that we would reach the end if we followed the markers. We could have easily gone off the well-worn path to explore something new, exciting, or unknown, but creating our own trail may have also gotten us lost, turned around, or far from our destination.

When God calls us to work—in an office, in our homes, with our families, around the country, online, down the street, mornings, afternoons, or nights—He has a purpose and a reason for it. These are the trail markers God uses to guide you to His final destination. You have not been overlooked or forgotten, and you are not lost. God knows where you are in this season, and He knows your heart.

Matthew 10:27-32 tells us, "What I tell you in the dark, speak in the light. What you hear in a whisper, proclaim on the housetops… Aren't two sparrows sold for a penny? Yet not one of them falls to the ground without your Father's consent. But even the hairs of your head have all been counted. So don't be afraid therefore; you are worth more than many sparrows."

What God has spoken to you in the light should not be doubted in the dark. He knows you, He has called you, and He has a plan for you. Not a single thing will happen without His consent. Do not be afraid.

It's easy to say, but we know it's not simple to live. What happens when life turns crazy upside down and nothing feels at peace? When I was fired from the only career I'd ever known, I was afraid. When I accepted a job that required frequent travel away from my family, flying to new places by myself, I was anxious. When I was asked to resign from that position and was removed from a community I loved, I was devastated.

I would be lying to say I believed 100 percent in my soul that God had something good planned to come out of that. All I could feel was doubt and fear. But God is faithful, and He stayed with me in those dark moments, carrying me when I didn't think I could take another step, send another resume, and recreate myself yet again.

I had to learn to give myself grace on the days when I just didn't know how I was going to do one more thing. I had to start writing down all the ways God had come through for me in the past as reminders that He had done it before and He would do it again. I had believed for so long that success meant only victory, but then I realized that, in God's economy, failures can be a success when we allow God to use them for our growth.

God knows every hair on your head, every doubt in your heart, every fear in your mind. But He has called you to your place, in your season, to serve Him. He doesn't want you to execute your job perfectly, but He does want you to seek Him, abide with Him, and trust Him.

God has made some promises to you, and He will keep them. Nothing about how we do any of the dozens of jobs we all accomplish, all the hats we all wear, or all the perceived successes or failures will ever change His character. He keeps promises.

As we go into the world with our new version of hustle, working hard to bring God glory, outdoing one another in honor, and serving instead of striving, we will stand out. We'll be working differently, prioritizing people over programs and projects, and we will be noticed. It's up to us to make sure the spotlight stays on God and what He's done in our lives.

Several years ago I found myself "all in" on a popular writing topic that told readers that my story matters and your story matters and her story matters! We all matter! At the time, it felt right. Based on Revelation 12:11, it was a call for women to be bold in sharing their stories because the Enemy is defeated "by the blood of the Lamb and by the word of their testimony."

May I share an unpopular opinion? I think that Scripture is perfect but the phrase I applied to it at the time is wrong. I think we've seen it as justification for our striving, our attempts to build platforms and grab the spotlight, because everyone is telling us our stories matter. We expect people to be there to hear our stories, receive our messages, and applaud our efforts because we've made it about us. But it's not your story that matters, or mine. It's God's story. It's the blood of the Lamb and our testimonies about what God has done in us and through us that matter. We should be loudly proclaiming God's mercy, forgiveness, and salvation to a world that needs to hear some good news, not using our stories to compete, compare, or climb ladders of success.

The work of God in our lives, the way He shines through the cracks, broken pieces, and weak spots, allows us to be a light through the work we do for His kingdom.

Matthew 5:14-16 tells us, "You are the light of the world. A city situated on a hill cannot be hidden. No one lights a lamp and puts it under a basket, but rather on a lampstand, and it gives light for all who are in the house. In the same way, let your light shine before men, so that they may see your good works and give glory to your Father in heaven." Do not be ashamed of the gifts, talents, and work God has given you to do. You are there for a reason, to be a light—not the recipient of the spotlight, but the beam that shines back to God.

I've never been to Israel, but my friend Annie has. In her book *Craving Connection*, she shares this story about that same Scripture passage, Matthew 5:14-16:

> In 2014 I visited Israel for the first time and walked up the Mount of Beatitudes to where Jesus preached these exact words to a crowd gathered near Him. I saw how, as you look across the terrain of that area, you can see little patches of homes, little cities literally built on the sides of hills. And I imagined, in that moment, what it was like to see them at night. That same yellow hue of candlelight in homes, clustered together to form a community…It feels like [Jesus] wasn't just asking us to be a light, to stand bright and alone like a lighthouse. I don't even think He was saying for us to be a lamp, necessarily. When I picture this scene He's describing, I picture a group of women sitting around, after the chores were finished for the day, laughing and reminiscing by candlelight. Because the lamp isn't hidden under a bowl, it lights the whole house, giving light to everyone gathered there. It's inviting. It's welcoming. It's friendly."[1]

This little light of mine isn't meant to be hidden. It's meant to be a beacon that guides others toward Jesus. It's meant to be a source of hope, comfort, and welcome. The work God has given you is a light you can use to gather others together in friendship and community. Whether you do it through hospitality, homeschooling, mentoring, managing a business, creating art, answering phones, delivering mail, writing books, preaching, making food, cleaning homes, or any other place God has you, you can shine right where you are.

---

*Holy hustle means using your light to brighten the
lives of others while shining the spotlight on God.*

Let's look at a few other Scripture verses that talk about light:

- The LORD went ahead of them in a pillar of cloud to lead
  them on their way during the day and in a pillar of fire to
  give them light at night, so that they could travel day or
  night (Exodus 13:21).

- He reveals mysteries from the darkness and brings the
  deepest darkness into the light (Job 12:22).

- LORD, You light my lamp; my God illuminates my darkness (Psalm 18:28).

- The LORD is my light and my salvation—whom should
  I fear? The LORD is the stronghold of my life—of whom
  should I be afraid? (Psalm 27:1).

- Your word is a lamp for my feet and a light on my path
  (Psalm 119:105).

- The sun will no longer be your light by day, and the bright-
  ness of the moon will not shine on you; but the LORD will
  be your everlasting light, and your God will be your splen-
  dor (Isaiah 60:19).

- Anyone who lives by the truth comes to the light, so that
  his works may be shown to be accomplished by God (John
  3:21).

- Then Jesus spoke to them again: "I am the light of the
  world. Anyone who follows Me will never walk in the
  darkness but will have the light of life" (John 8:12).

- You were once darkness, but now you are light in the Lord.
  Walk as children of light—for the fruit of the light results

in all goodness, righteousness, and truth—discerning what is pleasing to the Lord (Ephesians 5:8-10).

- You are a chosen race, a royal priesthood, a holy nation, a people for His possession, so that you may proclaim the praises of the One who called you out of darkness into His marvelous light (1 Peter 2:9).

The word *light* appears more than 270 times in the Bible, starting in the first chapter of Genesis and included in the final chapter of Revelation. God creates light, He is light, and He will be the only light we need. Just as it can be easy to layer our expectations and agendas over a phrase like *your story matters*, we can fall into the same trap if we believe only that we are a "light to the world" and forget that God has put us in that position to tell others our accomplishments are because of His work in our lives. We are not lights to promote ourselves or burn brighter than our neighbors. We are symbols of hope, safe places to land on hard days, and friends who love deeply. God lights our lamps, guides our steps, and banishes the darkness. We just need to be obedient to follow, humble to do the work, and gracious to include others.

∘∘∘∘∘∘∘∘∘∘∘∘∘∘∘∘∘∘∘∘∘ *Digging Deeper* ∘∘∘∘∘∘∘∘∘∘∘∘∘∘∘∘∘∘∘∘∘∘∘

Read Matthew 5

I hope you imagined yourself on that mountainside Annie described as you read this chapter of Scripture. If you've never looked up pictures or maps of this area of the world, take some time to see what you can find. Imagine yourself sitting on the grass, or maybe on a rock. You see hills in the distance and feel the breeze from the water below. You would be familiar with the stories of the Old Testament, so seeing Jesus, whom many considered the "new Moses," speak from a mountain would have provided "yet another parallel with the ancient Moses."[2]

Think of these connections Jesus's audience may have been considering. As Matthew Henry wrote, "Christ preached this sermon, which was an exposition of the law, upon a mountain, because upon a mountain the law was given; and this was also a solemn promulgation of the Christian law. But observe the difference: when the law was given, the Lord came down upon the mountain; now the Lord went up: then, he spoke in thunder and lightning; now, in a still small voice: then the people were ordered to keep their distance; now they are invited to draw near: a blessed change!"[3]

Ready to draw near?

Reading Matthew 5:14-16 has always caused me to pause. Much like holy hustle, the verses seem countercultural. Everything we're used to hearing tells us the confident, the happy, the strong, and the fighters are who win. But Jesus has a different message for those gathered on the mountainside. Matthew Henry's commentary notes that the point of this sermon was to help the disciples know the significance of what they had been called to do, who they were as followers of Christ, and how to accomplish the work. Understanding who we are and what we must do is the basis of how we work, how we hustle, and how we love others.

Jesus had recently performed countless miracles in Galilee, so those who came to hear Him were ready to hear instructions "from one in whom there appeared so much of a divine power and goodness."[4] Immediately going against our expectations for what we might consider essentials for success, Jesus shared that it was those who "cried out for God's help, depended entirely on Him for their needs, had a humble and contrite spirit, experienced His deliverance, and enjoyed His undeserved favor."[5] It's a blessing to be humble, to be comforted, and to be gentle. "The gentle are those who stubbornly trust God and surrender to His authority even when they cannot make sense of their circumstances."[6]

In those moments of uncertainty in our circumstances, it is so encouraging to know that we don't need to fight or strive. We can cling stubbornly to God, trusting He has a plan beyond anything we could ask for or imagine. And when it feels like everything or everyone is against us, how we choose to respond (with gentleness or as peacemakers) may not feel like the easy or rewarding choice. But Jesus promises that, as for the prophets and disciples who have gone before us, our reward in heaven will be great.

As challenging as the Beatitudes are for me to understand at times, this next section of Matthew 5 is one I love. "If the salt should lose its taste, how can it be made salty?" Jesus asks in verse 13. I get it. Who wants to season their food with something that has gone bad? At that point, the salt is only good for sprinkling on the ground to kill weeds, unseen, walked over. If we want to be useful in our work and as followers of Christ, we need to remain rooted in God's Word, refreshed and renewed. Otherwise, "Nothing grows where [we] go."[7]

We've all experienced the spreading of bad salt as jealousy, envy, or anger has been our lifestyle of choice. Nothing good comes from those seasons. Everything we work on is useless, pointing to ourselves far more often than to Jesus. Our lives and our work can be used in so many wonderful ways to grow the kingdom of God, but only once we're ready and willing to throw away the old salt and make room for something new.

In the same way, hiding our lights doesn't do anyone any good. Matthew 5:14-16 is our reminder that, as we are lights in the world, we are extensions of Jesus's ministry, representatives of the good news, and a gift that has been given to us by God. What a generous gift, indeed.

Further in Matthew 5 we find Jesus sharing how we are to respond to offense and our enemies. In every job I've ever had, from my work at a local music store as a teen to the freelance work I do now, some people have been challenging to work with. I've worked with people who stole inventory, girls who lied about me to gain sympathy from other employees, a woman who kept an espresso machine in her office but refused to share if you weren't part of her select group of friends, and women who gossiped about me behind my back. God knew we would be, well, human. We all make mistakes, and sometimes our salt loses its flavor. Instead of leaving us to figure it all out on our own, He gave us clear instructions.

Matthew 5:38-42 instructs us how to deal with those who insult or hurt us. I've tried doing things my way, returning the offense with an equal offense, or taking part in gossip to try to make myself feel better, but none of that grew anything healthy. It only hid the light God gave me under an ugly basket that caused me extra pain in the end.

Jesus shows us a different way, instructing us to turn the other cheek (Matthew 5:39), give more than what's being asked of us (5:40), and go the extra mile (5:41). Jesus was speaking specifically against retaliation and teaching His disciples how to deal with their oppressors, but I think we can apply the lessons to our work as well. I'm sure some people in the spaces where we've been called to serve could benefit from the results of this kind of generous response. It's easy to outdo someone in honor when we're getting along with the person, but imagine the restored relationships that might come out of going the extra mile with those whom we struggle to love.

This chapter in Matthew ends with what might very well be one of the hardest things for us to do—love our enemies. Maybe your enemy is your next-door neighbor who complains about everything you do. We've had noisy college neighbors, an apartment neighbor who loved his early morning jazzercise routine, neighbors who kept track of how often we had friends and family visit, and neighbors who picked on every little change we made to our home. It's easy to close yourself off after experiences like that. We've lived in our current home for nearly ten years, and only in the last year have we begun to connect with the families on our street. We realized we weren't humble about our past mistakes, and we were angry with the actions of our neighbors. It felt unfair, and they seemed like the enemy.

We also realized we not only couldn't expect our daughter to love the kids at school who weren't always nice to her, but couldn't honestly answer her when she asked why we didn't talk to our neighbors. Just as we want our children to model their behavior on what they learn at home, God wants us to reflect Him in our actions (Matthew 5:45).

Not by our silent treatments, our gossip, our anger, or our bitterness will we be known as Christians, but by our love and the light we shine as a result of the work God is doing in our lives. Be a bright light to those who need one most, wherever you are called to serve God's kingdom.

Holy Hustle Story

WYNTER: MINISTRY LEADER

Within a five-year period I became the mother of four daughters! It was a crazy, hectic time, and in all honesty, I was having a hard time finding joy or contentment in the season. I now realize I was striving. I didn't want to be "just an at-home mom." I wanted more, but I was trying to find it and achieve it on my own. It wasn't until I surrendered and focused on serving the people scattered around my house that God was able to use that exact experience to push me into my holy hustle.

For me, holy hustle means being fully committed and focused on serving God through my actions, regardless of the details or specific circumstance. When I discover the joy of the work God has called me to do slipping away, I focus on Luke 10:27: "Love the Lord your God with all your heart, with all your soul, and with all your strength, and with all your mind; and your neighbor as yourself."

Reflection

As we wrap up this section on work and enter into a conversation about what it looks like to not only work hard but rest well, take some time to reflect on one of the verses shared earlier about "light," or open your Bible to find one that resonates with your heart. Spend time with God, asking Him to illuminate the places in your life that have felt dark, to show you where you've strayed from His path for you, and the times recently when you've worked for your glory instead of His. Write down several ways you can be a light to your family, your neighbors, or your coworkers this week, using the gifts God has given you to show others His mercy, grace, and love.

◇◇◇◇◇

_____

_____

_____

_____

_____

_____

_____

_____

_____

_____

_____

_____

_____

_____

_____

_____

The Blessing of Rest

Work is a blessing. God has so arranged the world that work is necessary, and He gives us hands and strength to do it. The enjoyment of leisure would be nothing if we had only leisure. It is the joy of work well done that enables us to enjoy rest, just as it is the experiences of hunger and thirst that make food and drink such pleasures.

ELISABETH ELLIOT

sat in my counselor's office, feet tucked up on a recliner, a soft blanket draped across the armrest. I didn't know where to begin telling this stranger what I'd been struggling with over the past few months—the anxiety, sleeplessness, sense of loss and failure, and fears of worthlessness. I was burned out in a big way. From the outside, it looked like I'd been living a dream life. Writing, speaking, traveling, working for a ministry, hosting events, and even recording a video that put my face (larger than life) on the big screen at several massive Christian women's events. I'd made it. And I was as miserable as I'd been when I was fired from that corporate career.

With kindness and the wisdom that comes from having lived through similar seasons, my counselor pointed out I needed to rest—not only rest to recover from a series of highly stressful years, but to make rest part of my daily routine. She encouraged me to think about the last time I felt truly relaxed, to close my eyes and relive that moment. What did it smell like, sound like, feel like? Was it at the beach, listening to the waves crash, or was it by a fireplace with a good book and a cup of coffee, snuggled under a blanket? When life felt overwhelming and my to-do list started to bring feelings of anxiety, she told me to spend 30 seconds simply escaping to that place.

I nodded, but mentally rolled my eyes.

I didn't have a place to go, a memory I could pull out and escape to in those moments. Our family vacations for years had included work, and even our holidays were interspersed with small projects, checking email, putting out social media fires. How was I supposed to escape to a place that didn't exist? Although I couldn't take her advice immediately, it did make me more aware of a gap in my life. Working hard? I could do that. But resting well? I had no idea what that looked like, yet I knew I wanted to create those experiences with my family so we could all draw on them in our busy seasons.

We are about to wrap up our journey with encouragement to do the same thing God did when He finished His work at creation: rest. Let's dig deeper and explore the difference between rest and laziness, why rest is essential, and how our work, our service, and our rest work together to create a sustainable model of holy hustle.

The "work hard" side of this new concept of hustle is easy for me, but this part? Learning how to rest well? That has taken a lot more time, practice, and trust. I've had to admit some prideful thoughts to God as He's asked me to incorporate rest into my life. Thoughts like:

- *No one else can do this as well as I can.*

- *If I don't do it, who will?*

- *If I say yes to all these projects I'll have job security.*

- *I don't have time to rest.*

Whether it's about the work I need to do to maintain our household for my family, the tasks on my freelance to-do list, or the commitments I've made to friends, my pride tells me I need to strive, work harder than everyone else, and prove I'm irreplaceable. In reality all that does is cause me to experience burnout and frustration. It also causes a lack of the joy, joy that can be found only in living within our calling—and the boundaries—God has created for us. My pride says stepping away from work or social media means someone else will step in and take over, or that I'll be forgotten. God tells me rest is necessary, part of the blessing we can experience when we work hard for His glory.

Parts of my job require me to spend quite a bit of time on social media, and I love it. I find community on those pages and apps, and it's one of my favorite ways to share the messages God has put on my heart. But something beautiful happens when I walk away from social media for a weekend. This idea of chasing Sabbath, finding moments throughout our weekend to settle our hearts and do things that bring us joy, brings clarity and peace. When most of my time is spent surrounded by the cacophony of all-caps excitement and hashtags about *all the things*, my heart becomes quickly absorbed in making sure what I'm doing/saying/writing looks good. In my line of work, I need to be noticed to succeed. We call it a "platform"—the way someone will pay attention to you because your work stands out from the rest.

But when I walk away from it all for a few days to enjoy real-life community, the hustle fades and hope remains. Might God want me to do all those things? He might. But none of the references I found in Scripture described "platforms" the way we talk about them. In 2 Chronicles 5:14, Solomon stands on a platform to kneel before God and invite Him into the temple they build for Him. It wasn't about the brilliant prayer Solomon prayed. No one in attendance took notes about what he said, tweeted it, or had a "fear of missing out" moment. Instead they witnessed "the glory of the Lord" fill the house. The Holy Spirit was elevated, not a single person in attendance.

In Nehemiah 8:5, Ezra stands on a platform to read the Word of God to a crowd hungry to understand Scripture. And he didn't stand alone. It wasn't about what Ezra was doing, what he was wearing, or what kind of popularity contest he won to earn the opportunity. He read, and the people stood to honor God. The Word of God was elevated, not Ezra.

Do you want to know when "platform" was used in a way that most resembles the way we think of it? In Acts 12, Herod stands on a platform and makes a speech. The crowd goes wild over his words, and he fails to give God glory. The result? He's struck down with a flesh-eating disease and dies.

If the result of self-glorification on a platform built on my achievements leads to that kind of end, I'm out. No thank you. Bottom line? There's no "I" in platform. It's never meant to be about us. What if we used the places and platforms God gifts us as places to elevate Him, His Word, and His good news? What if we got to work only after asking God to hide us completely, inviting Him to take center stage? What if we used social media, our neighborhoods, cubicles, and gathering spaces as places to invite the glory of the Lord to fill the house?

What if we took the "I" out of platform?

We can model for others what it means to live a life that honors God in our work, whatever that looks like. We can offer encouragement with the words we share and the comments we leave for others as we choose to cheer for them instead of competing against them. And we can take breaks, rest awhile, and live a life worth sharing about when we stop putting our faith in our online presence and put it back in the One who will never fail us, who never forgets us, and who will always listen to us.

When it comes to holy hustle, we need to rest.

It feels counterintuitive, doesn't it? After all, we've been talking throughout the book about the worth of our work, working hard after the calling God has placed on our lives, outdoing one another in honor. So why rest?

Unlike with the world's version of hustle, we rest because we follow the model of work God showed us in the beginning. In Genesis 1 and 2 we read how God created the world out of nothing—every living creature, man, and woman was created in six days. And on the seventh day God rested.

If rest isn't too good for God, why do we act like we don't have time for it?

We need time away from our work so we can refill, refuel, and refresh our spirits. Instead of pouring out all the time, we need to discover ways to be filled up and allow others to serve in their gifts in our lives. And we need to be in the Word.

Rest is hard for me because my natural inclination is to hustle and strive. I've lived long enough with my flaws to understand that, buried deep inside, I believe if I'm not working, I'm failing. And if I'm failing, I'm worthless. But in the same way I believe we can serve God in our work, I believe we honor Him when we rest.

We need to slow down, spend time in the Word, and be quiet enough to hear God's voice so we are better equipped to do the work He's calling us to do. When I try to go 24/7 without a break, not only do I burn out, neglect my family, and serve as a poor steward of my health, but I start to make hurried decisions based on my agenda and dreams instead of listening to God's quiet guidance.

Charles Swindoll wrote, "God never asked us to meet life's pressures and demands on our own terms or by relying upon our own strength. Nor did He demand that we win His favor by assembling an impressive portfolio of good deeds. Instead, He invites us to enter His rest."[1]

God worked and called it good,
and He rested and called it holy.

We are invited to join Him in that rest, because in those moments we can lay down our burdens, abide with Him, and do what He created us to do to refresh our souls for the coming days.

Rest, for me, used to look like sitting on the sofa and mindlessly snacking while watching television. I thought I deserved that break, that doing "nothing" was how I was supposed to relax. But I often felt more exhausted, gross from all the sugar I'd consumed, and completely unmotivated to do anything at all. May I bust a myth for you? Rest looks different for everyone. I have friends who are energized by a long morning run where they can be alone with their thoughts, prayers, and the pavement. I have other friends who are rejuvenated by gathering people in their home for good food and great conversation. And you might find you are at your best rest when you're reading a book, creating art, playing music, or gardening.

God has created us with such care that there should be no surprise our rest can be as unique as our work.

My husband and I are both in fields that require us to spend a lot of time thinking, teaching, and reading—which means that the balance, for us, is to spend time doing something with our hands. During his summer break, my husband spends most of his time outside, maintaining our home, doing yard work, and with tasks like building fences and installing patios. I've found a love for creating beautiful spaces outside with flowers, digging my hands (glove-covered, because *bugs*) into the dirt. And I've discovered I can rest well when I spend time with my family on the weekends, creating experiences and memories we'll all remember. Trips to Hersheypark, hiking, visiting Gettysburg, or taking a short trip to spend the day with family keeps us off our devices and screens and invested in one another. We laugh more, and we sleep well at the end of those days.

But we've found rest in those activities only because we seek God in them. We thank Him for His creation as we work on the piece of land He's given us to steward. We get to know one another, our dreams, and our prayer needs as we travel together in a car on a short trip. Rest doesn't need to look like a quiet room with a scented candle and in-depth Bible study to be restorative to your soul. When I try to make "rest" fit into some box that looks like what someone else is doing, I end up either frustrated or lazy.

Just as striving is the "gone too far" side of serving, laziness is the "gone too far" side of rest. We need rest. But our rest has a purpose. It's not meant to be an excuse to avoid work. Sabbath is a day set aside, a time to walk with the Lord in prayer. It's when we can thank Him for the work we've been given and seek His will for what's to come. Time to rest—whether it's at the end of each day when you close your office door, on the weekends with your family, or on a day you choose to dedicate to time with God—isn't meant to be a time of inactivity, but a time of intentional connection with God.

When you look at the way you've been trying to incorporate rest into your life, do you feel like you've slipped too far into laziness? Or has rest never even entered the picture? What would it look like for you to rest in a way that breathes life into your weary heart but also honors God? Our work can be a blessing to those we serve, and our rest is a blessing—a gift—as well.

When we are well rested, we can make better decisions, serve in our full strength, and better handle all that comes our way. Those unexpected detours in our journey won't feel as terrifying or frustrating when we can approach them after time spent abiding with God. When I'm striving or being lazy, I'm trusting in my abilities to make things happen or my feelings of prideful righteousness that I "deserve" something more than what I have. When I'm working hard and resting well, I'm trusting God to direct my days, protect my reputation, and open the right doors in His timing.

When we've taken the time to lay down our work and intentionally seek the kind of rest God created us to enjoy, we're able to pass those blessings along to those He has put in our lives. We can model rest to our families, we can prioritize people over projects, and we can enter our work ready to serve with our whole hearts. We can also create a sustainable model of holy hustle that allows us to do the best possible work for God's kingdom as we choose to intentionally work hard, rest well, and repeat.

As we wrap up our holy hustle journey, I want to share something I believe about all the work God has called us to do. You and me? We are called to take the gospel to the far ends of the earth and to be a light on a hilltop, and we can do that right where God has called us. What if we saw our work as our mission field?

What if we decided to commit to where we've been called?

I don't know how to explain this fire that thought starts in my heart.

And I don't know why I feel so strongly that I need to invite you to join me. But I do need to invite you. I need to know I'm not the only one who lives her faith every day feeling ready to take her holy hustle to the next level.

It's time to stand firm.

> Rise up and shine, for your light has come. The shining-greatness of the Lord has risen upon you. For see, darkness will cover the earth. Much darkness will cover the people. But the Lord will rise upon you, and His shining-greatness will be seen upon you. Nations will come to your light. And kings will see the shining-greatness of the Lord on you (Isaiah 60:1-3 NLV).

It's time to stop talking the good talk and start the walk. It's time to stop *saying* we don't want to compare ourselves to anyone and stop *doing* it. It's time to lean into the work and season and place God has given us, embrace them with both arms, feet planted firmly beneath us, and say, "Here I am."

> My beloved spoke and said to me,
>   "Arise, my darling,
>   my beautiful one, come with me.
> See! The winter is past;
>   the rains are over and gone.
> Flowers appear on the earth;
>   the season of singing has come,
> the cooing of doves
>   is heard in our land (Song of Songs 2:10-12 NIV).

It's time to step out of our comfortable hibernation and do what God is calling us to do, whether it looks popular or like what anyone else is already doing. Do it anyway. Be weird for Jesus. It's time to stop waiting to feel qualified and remember that God has not come to serve the healthy but to heal the sick. When it's time for us to embrace who He created us to be, He will equip us with everything we need.

Whether it looks like what we planned, whether we feel like we can do it, when God calls us to rise, to stand, to move, to do the work for His kingdom that will be fruitful, He will not leave us to do it alone.

> You will not have to fight this battle. Take up your positions; stand firm and see the deliverance the LORD will give you, Judah and Jerusalem. Do not be afraid; do not be discouraged. Go out to face them tomorrow, and the LORD will be with you (2 Chronicles 20:17 NIV).

Stand firm. Let go of the titles and the hats you wear and the carefully arranged agendas. Realize that your battle isn't with one another, but with the Enemy, and choose to reach over and grab the hand of the woman beside you, the one coming after you, or the one a few steps ahead of you, and rise up—together. Fight the good fight, together—not against one another. Work hard, rest well, and outdo one another in honor.

Cheer, encourage, rebuke, teach, train, love, support—one another.

> Finally, be strong in the Lord and in his mighty power. Put on the full armor of God, so that you can take your stand against the devil's schemes. For our struggle is not against flesh and blood, but against the rulers, against the authorities, against the powers of this dark world and against the spiritual forces of evil in the heavenly realms. Therefore put on the full armor of God, so that when the day of evil comes, you may be able to stand your ground, and after you have done everything, to stand (Ephesians 6:10-13 NIV).

Be who God created you to be. Live it boldly. Stand where you've been called. Get free from your expectations and stay free in the knowledge that the work we do for the kingdom—when we get on our feet and move when God calls us—will bear fruit. That will leave a legacy.

> As Jesus went on from there, he saw a man named Matthew sitting at the tax collector's booth. "Follow me," he told him, and Matthew got up and followed him (Matthew 9:9 NIV).

Follow Him. Stand firm.

Digging Deeper

Read Psalm 46

It might be a little selfish of me, but I want to end our time together with my favorite passage in Scripture—Psalm 46. This is the psalm I personally turn to when I find myself straying from the holy hustle path God has given me. The Psalms are such a beautiful representation of life, from the joy and the struggles, to the celebrations and frustrations, to gratitude and grief. And through it all, the author (or it might be authors) turns to God.

Although they cover a multitude of messages, the Psalms are a "record of the responses of God's people in worship and prayer" and "serves the purpose of teaching us how to relate to God in various circumstances of life. The psalms also demonstrate God's sovereignty and goodness for His people in order to instill confidence in those who trust Him."[2]

One of the ways God speaks most clearly to me is through music—often through worship music, but occasionally He will draw me closer to Him through songs I hear that simply remind me of His faithfulness or His nearness. Psalm 46 is meant to be a song, and although the poetic nature of the Scripture is certainly beautiful, I imagine it would be stunning when sung in its original language. Singing is not one of the gifts God has given me, so I will happily enjoy reading the words.

As we explore the idea of rest, I can't help but be drawn to the very beginning of this psalm: "God is our refuge and strength" (verse 1). He is there for us when even the most stable, secure places in our lives are shaken and unsteady. A refuge is a place of safety, an opportunity for relief, protection, or aid,[3] and it's comforting to think of God in that way. After long hours of serving and living out our holy hustle, what a gift it is to know we can turn to God for rest and relief. As we stay firm in God's presence, taking the time to abide with Him and seek His will, Psalm 46 encourages us that "God is within her; she will not be toppled" (verse 5). Work is hard, and life is unpredictable, but when we stay on the path God has created for us, we can walk forward with sure, steady steps.

If you have a Bible app on your phone or are near a computer, pull up Psalm 46 and read it in several different translations. Psalm 46:10 has long been my favorite Scripture verse, and I love the different ways it can be read:

- Stop your fighting—and know that I am God (HCSB).

- Step out of the traffic! Take a long, loving look at me, your High God (MSG).

- Be still and know (recognize, understand) that I am God (AMP).

- Be still, be calm, see, and understand I am the True God (VOICE).

- Be still, and know that I am God (ESV).

Regardless of the translation you choose, the message is this: slow down. Remember who God is and that it's not your job to do His job. I remember reading this Scripture with a youth group I was volunteering with and realizing this verse is so beautifully written that it makes sense even when we break it down, piece by piece.

Be.
Be still.
Be still and know.
Be still and know that I am.
Be still and know that I am God.

We can be still and rest well because God is the I Am, the beginning and the end, the Alpha and the Omega. He gave us His model of work and rest at the start of creation, and He continues to be active, working in our lives and inviting us to enjoy that same rest today.

The work is good, and the rest is holy. Be still.

Holy Hustle Story

ANGELA: CEO

One ironic way God has redeemed the hustle of my life is by giving me two business partners (and best friends) who are nothing like me. The process of learning to depend on other people and not cater to my personal "drive" and preference for autonomy has been a refining fire that I've both despised and desired. Working, building, and dreaming with other people isn't my forte, and I've always considered hustle to be a one-person job. But God created a vision in my heart that I alone could not build. He created in me a *need* for others who would bring the skills and strengths I lacked. This union/partnership forced me to share my hustle (which initially felt like running with an anchor tied around my waist), but looking back, I can see how reducing, distributing, and equalizing my hustle gave way to increased vision, focus, energy, and strength. We aren't meant to hustle alone.

Holy hustle is all about pace. I believe if you find the right pace in each season, you can run without growing weary. In some seasons the pace is faster, busier, and more hurried. In others, the pace is slow, deliberate, and carefully chosen. Too often we're sprinting a marathon or jogging a 100-meter dash. That kind of hustle leads to failure, exhaustion, and frustration. The holy kind of hustle feels sustainable, meaningful, and victorious.

Romans 8:28 is always a great centering Scripture for me, especially in the context of hustle. Knowing that He's working all things together for good means I can unclench my fists and loosen my grip on things I'm trying to control. Holy hustle comes with ups and downs, highs and lows, good and bad, and knowing that all of it is in His control and for His glory brings immediate perspective to every situation.

Reflection

Make a list of things that bring your heart joy or rest. Maybe catching up on your favorite television show is on that list. Or maybe you feel rejuvenated after having coffee with a friend, walking in the park, taking an art class, or exploring a new town. Maybe you need to reintroduce naptime into your life or spend an hour at the local library. This is the time to make the kind of "treat yourself" list that isn't self-centered, but God-centered.

Ask God to show you how He has created you to rest—ignoring how social media, books, or your friends say you *should* do it. Choose one item from your list to incorporate into your schedule this week, putting boundaries on your work and making time to truly rest. Put your faith, identity, and worth in Christ alone as you lay aside your pride, agenda, and fears. Rest well.

Final Commissioning

Here is my final prayer for you and me as we embrace holy hustle. With every ordinary act of obedience, may we honor God with our service. As we work, eat, exercise, write, speak, discipline, encourage, and worship, may every act of our lives be about God and not ourselves. May our work, our right-here faith, and our called-to-this-place-on-purpose life be an offering to God that brings even a little bit of His kingdom to earth.

> *Father, help us to be weird for You. May we embrace our place when it doesn't quite fit in, working to stay humble rather than highly exalted. You are to be exalted, honored, and glorified. Help us stay fixed on You, standing firm in our belief that You will use every door, every task, every vocation, and every location to help us grow to be more like You.*
>
> *When we find ourselves striving, bring us back to You, Jesus. May we remember that every gift comes from You. May our work be our act of service to You, shining a light in the dark corners of the world that draws others not to our own fame, but to Your salvation and love.*

Help us remember that our work is not about us, but for You.

Help us to work hard, love others, and rest well. When life gets hard and things don't go our way, may we turn to You in prayer instead of trying to fix it on our own. When we doubt where You've called us, the gifts You've given us, or our worth, may we turn to Your Word to be reminded that we are loved and chosen, and that You do not make mistakes.

Thank You, Lord, for allowing us to be Your hands, feet, and heart here on earth. May the work of our hands and the words we speak be a gift back to You.

Amen.

◇◇◇◇◇

Holy Hustle Story Bios

Clare Smith: Clare lives with her husband and two children in Northeast Ohio. Her passion, outside of nurturing her children and home, is motivating women of all ages and stages of life to live well physically, emotionally, and spiritually. Visit her at claresmith.me or connect on Instagram @claresmithofficial.

Erin Mohring: Erin lives with her husband and their three sons in Nebraska, where she enjoys running, reading, and eating popcorn. You can connect with her on her personal blog, homewiththeboys.net, and on all social media at @homewiththeboys. (Instagram is her favorite.)

Jennifer Dukes Lee: Jennifer is a storyteller and a grace dweller. She and her husband, Scott, live on the Lee Family Farm in Northwest Iowa, where they spend at least five minutes every day in the pursuit of happiness. She is the author of *The Happiness Dare* and *Love Idol*. Jennifer blogs about faith and life at JenniferDukesLee.com. You can connect with her on Twitter @dukeslee.

Bri McKoy: Bri is a writer and home cook. She is the owner and writer for her blog, OurSavoryLife.com, a food blog with recipes and stories from around her table, and the author of *Come and Eat: A Celebration of Love and Grace Around the Everyday Table*. You can connect with Bri on Instagram @brimckoy.

Hayley Morgan: Hayley is a writer, speaker, and entrepreneur who inspires women to create lives with more passion and less fuss. Her first book, *Wild and Free,* cowritten with Jess Connolly, was published in May 2016 and quickly became a *USA Today* bestseller. She and her husband started Wildly Co., an ethical children's clothing line, and she is also the cofounder of the Influence Conference and Network. Hayley lives in Indianapolis, Indiana, with her husband and their four sons. She blogs at thetinytwig.com and hayleyemorgan.com.

Kate Battistelli: Kate is the author of *Growing Great Kids: Partner with God to Cultivate His Purpose in Your Child's Life,* mom to Grammy–award winning artist Francesca Battistelli, and Mimi to Francesca's children. She's been married to Mike for 33 years and blogs about food and faith at KateBattistelli.com. You can follow her on Instagram @katebatistelli.

Erin Weidemann: Erin is a teacher turned professional author. A former college athlete, Erin is also a five-time cancer survivor. She lives in Encinitas, California, with her husband, Brent, and their daughter, Rooney. In addition to being the cofounder and CEO of Bible Belles (biblebelles.com), Erin is the host of the *Heroes For Her* podcast. You can connect with her on Instagram @biblebelles.

Andrea Howey: Andrea resides in Dallas and uses hand lettering to encourage hearts, strengthen faith, and point people to Jesus. By simply sharing her heart and lettering messages of hope, truth, and faith from the Word of God, she aims to encourage the God-given courage in others so they can rise out of fear and insecurity, use the gifts God has put in their hands, and fulfill the unique and beautiful purpose, potential, and destiny God has for their lives. You can connect with Andrea on Instagram @andrearhowey.

Wynter Pitts: Wynter is the founder of *For Girls Like You,* a ministry to tween girls and their parents that includes a print magazine and other print and web resources. The mother of four beautiful girls, Alena (9),

Kaitlyn (6), and twins Olivia and Camryn (4), and the wife of ten years to Jonathan, Wynter fully understands and relates to the daily joys and challenges in marriage and family. Connect with Wynter at forgirlslikeyou.com or on Instagram @forgirlslikeyou.

Angela Beeler: Angela is founder and CEO of Refit® Revolution. The founders of REFIT® are dream-chasing with one goal in mind: to authentically love people through fitness and community. Inspired by their values and fueled by their faith, Angela, Catherine, and Emily have spent the last five years developing a fitness program that empowers, inspires, welcomes, and loves. You can connect with Angela at refitrev.com or on Instagram @angela_beeler.

Notes

Chapter 1—The Redemption of Hustle

1. Dictionary.com

2. Andreas J. Kostenberger, "Chapter Introduction," *Holman Christian Standard Bible* (Nashville, TN: Holman Bible Publishers, 2010), 2051.

3. https://www.biblegateway.com/resources/matthew-henry/Col.3.12-Col.3.17.

Chapter 2—A Good-bye Party for Striving

1. Emily P. Freeman, *Simply Tuesday* (Grand Rapids, MI: Revell, 2015), 73–74.

2. Myquillyn Smith, "Why No and Yes are BFFs," Blog, November, 2015http://thenester.com/2015/11/why-no-yes-are-bffs.html.

3. Joanna Weaver, *Having a Mary Heart in a Martha World* (Colorado Springs, CO: WaterBrook, 2000), 48–50.

4. David S. Dockery, "Circumstances of Writing," *Holman Christian Standard Bible* (Nashville, TN: Holman Bible Publishers, 2010), 2024.

5. David S. Dockery, "Chapter Introduction," *Holman Christian Standard Bible* (Nashville, TN: Holman Bible Publishers, 2010), 2024.

6. David S. Dockery, "Energeia," *Holman Christian Standard Bible* (Nashville, TN: Holman Bible Publishers, 2010), 2024, 2030.

7. Dictionary.com

8. David S. Dockery, "Ergon," *Holman Christian Standard Bible* (Nashville, TN: Holman Bible Publishers, 2010), 2024, 2030.

Chapter 3—Called Here

1. Jill Briscoe, "All the Way Home," IF Gathering, Austin, Texas, February 2017.

2. *Holman Christian Standard Bible* (Nashville, TN: Holman Bible Publishers, 2010), 1569.

3. *Holman Christian Standard Bible* (Nashville, TN: Holman Bible Publishers, 2010), 1570.

4. D. Brent Sandy, "Study Bible Notes," *Holman Christian Standard Bible* (Nashville, TN: Holman Bible Publishers, 2010), 1576.

Chapter 4—"Hello, Hustle"

1. *Holman Christian Standard Bible* (Nashville, TN: Holman Bible Publishers, 2010), 4 .

2. https://www.biblegateway.com/resources/matthew-henry/Gen.1.1-Gen.1.2.

3. https://www.biblegateway.com/resources/matthew-henry/Gen.2.1-Gen.2.3.

4. https://www.biblegateway.com/resources/matthew-henry/Gen.2.1-Gen.2.3.

Chapter 5—Harvesting the Blessing

1. Lara Casey, *Make It Happen* (Nashville, TN: W Publishing Group, 2014), 137–8.

2. https://www.biblegateway.com/resources/matthew-henry/Ruth.2.1-Ruth.2.3.

3. https://www.biblegateway.com/resources/matthew-henry/Ruth.2.1-Ruth.2.3.

Chapter 6—The Superpower of Service

1. John Ortberg, *All the Places to Go…How Will You Know?* (Wheaton, IL: Tyndale House Publishers, Inc., 2015), 24–25.

2. Ortberg, *All the Places to Go,* 15, 35.

3. Ortberg, *All the Places to Go,* 36.

4. Rebecca Faires, "She Fears the Lord," *She Reads Truth Bible* (Nashville, TN: Holman Bible Publishers, 2017), 1061.

5. David K. Stabnow, "Study Bible Notes," *Holman Christian Standard Bible* (Nashville, TN: Holman Bible Publishers, 2010), 1082.

6. Stabnow, "Study Bible Notes," 1082.

7. https://www.biblegateway.com/resources/matthew-henry/Prov.31.10-Prov.31.31.

8. https://www.biblegateway.com/resources/matthew-henry/Prov.31.10-Prov.31.31.

Chapter 7—Anything You Can Do, I Can Do Better

1. Jenn Sprinkle and Kelly Rucker, *31 Days of Prayer for the Dreamer and Doer* (Fort Worth, TX: NyreePress Literary Group, 2014), 76.

2. *Holman Christian Standard Bible* (Nashville, TN: Holman Bible Publishers, 2010), 1922.

3. @hstleandhrt, Instagram photo, May 4, 2017, https://www.instagram.com/p/BTqfcOcjs_7/?taken-by=hstlandhrt.

4. Edwin A. Blum, "Study Bible Notes," *Holman Christian Standard Bible* (Nashville, TN: Holman Bible Publishers, 2010), 1946.

5. Jill McDaniel, "Renewed Minds," *She Reads Truth Bible* (Nashville, TN: Holman Bible Publishers, 2017), 1920.

6. Blum, "Study Bible Notes," 1948.

Chapter 8—Choosing Community

1. Bob Goff, "We won't be distracted by comparison if we're captivated by purpose," Facebook, December 29, 2015, https://www.facebook.com/bobgoffis/posts/963422810399659.

2. Jenn Sprinkle and Kelly Rucker, *31 Days of Prayer for the Dreamer and Doer* (Fort Worth, TX: NyreePress Literary Group, 2014), 176.

3. Lara Casey, *Make It Happen* (Nashville, TN: W Publishing Group, 2014), 205.

4. Casey, *Make It Happen,* 206.

5. F. Alan Tomlinson, "Study Bible Notes," *Holman Christian Standard Bible* (Nashville, TN: Holman Bible Publishers, 2019), 1957.

6. Tomlinson, "Study Bible Notes," 1979.

7. Tomlinson, "Study Bible Notes," 1979.

8. https://www.biblegateway.com/resources/theology-of-work/gifted-communities-1-corinthians-12-1-14-40.

Chapter 9—This Little Light of Mine

1. Annie F. Downs, *Craving Connection* (Nashville, TN: B&H Publishing Group, 2017), 106–7.

2. Charles L. Quarles, "Study Bible Notes," *Holman Christian Standard Bible* (Nashville, TN: Holman Bible Publishers, 2010), 1617.

3. Matthew Henry, https://www.biblegateway.com/resources/matthew-henry/Matt.5.1-Matt.5.2.

4. Matthew Henry, https://www.biblegateway.com/resources/matthew-henry/Matt.5.1-Matt.5.2.

5. Quarles, "Study Bible Notes," 1618.

6. Quarles, "Study Bible Notes," 1618.

7. *Holman Christian Standard Bible* (Nashville, TN: Holman Bible Publishers, 2010), 1619.

Chapter 10—The Blessing of Rest

1. Charles R. Swindoll, *Jesus: The Greatest Life of All* (Nashville, TN: Thomas Nelson, 2008), 94.

2. Kevin R. Warstler, "Study Bible Notes," *Holman Christian Standard Bible* (Nashville, TN: Holman Bible Publishers, 2010), 879.

3. Dictionary.com.

Acknowledgments

I long believed I could make all my dreams and goals happen on my own, without help from anyone else. Next to salvation, the greatest gift I've received from God has been freedom from that lie. This journey to put *Holy Hustle* into your hands happened through the hard work, prayers, and trust of a community. My community.

With a tremendous amount of gratitude I offer thanks to:

Katrina, Janelle, Heidi, and Michelle for your constant support and for continuing to be my friend even when I wasn't the easiest friend to have. You loved me long before the internet knew me, and I will cherish your friendships forever.

My local Starbucks for keeping me fueled to do what I love most and never judging the goofy girl in the corner with her huge stacks of books, Bibles, and pens, grinning at her laptop. Thanks for making my daughter think I'm famous because I'm now a "regular."

Mom, for being the inspiration behind so much of this story. Everything I know about working hard to support my family, I learned from you.

My family, friends, life group, and church community for praying me through these pages. You never let my failures define me.

The wonderful team who believed in this message from the moment they heard it: my agent, Janet Grant, and my editor, Kathleen Kerr. You've made this dream come true.

To you, for picking up this book and trusting me to take you on this journey. That is a kindness I can never repay.

About the Author

A self-proclaimed "digital missionary," Crystal dreamed of her perfect career as climbing the corporate ladder and achieving success. And she did it, becoming an assistant vice president of marketing at a local community bank before her thirtieth birthday. But then God redefined hustle for her, taking Crystal on a journey from striving to serving. From that role in corporate America, to serving as a project manager for a web design company, to working as the editorial and marketing manager for (in)courage (a daily devotional blog run by DaySpring and read by women around the world), to using her talents as a communications coordinator at her church and a freelance communications consultant for a foster and adoption nonprofit based out of Austin, Texas, Crystal has understood the tempting pull of striving. But she has learned to lean into the blessing of focusing her hustle toward serving God's kingdom.

Through those changes, God has proven faithful to never waste an experience, connecting Crystal with friends, mentors, and influencers who have shown her what it means to cling to Jesus and His model for our lives in everything from friendship to work.

Now a self-employed mama to a six-year-old (and married to her high school sweetheart), Crystal is passionate about cultivating a community where faith and friendship come together. The author of *Creative Basics: 30 Days to Awesome Social Media Art*, cocreator of the "Clarity Coaching" course, editor and contributing author of *Craving Connection: 30 Challenges for Real Life Engagement* (B&H Books, 2017), and the host of the annual Write 31 Days challenge (serving more than two thousand writers each year), Crystal writes regularly at crystalstine.me. You can connect with her on Facebook at facebook.com/crystalstineofficial or on Instagram @crystalstine.

To learn more about Harvest House books and
to read sample chapters, visit our website:

www.harvesthousepublishers.com

HARVEST HOUSE PUBLISHERS
EUGENE, OREGON